D1195089

Navarro Baldeweg

Navarro Baldeweg

Juan Navarro Baldeweg

Gingko Press

Navarro Baldeweg

First published in English by
Gingko Press Inc.
5768 Paradise Drive, Suite J
Corte Madera, CA 94925, USA

For a catalog of books published by Gingko Press,
call 415 924 9615 or write to books@gingkopress.com
www.gingkopress.com

Publisher *Raúl Rispa*
English Editor *Erica Witschey*

English translation *Hawys Pritchard / David Cohn*
Interior layout *Ignacio Moreno Rodriguez /*
Maria José Chacartegui / Waldo Pérez Cino

Spanish edition for the Spanish language territories
published by Tanais Ediciones, Seville, Madrid
German edition for the German language territories
published by Gingko Press, Hamburg
Italian edition for the Italian language territories
published by Logos Art, Modena

Color reproduction and filmset by Proyectos Gráficos
Digitales, s.l., and Monterreina, s.a.
Printed by Monterreina, s.a., Madrid

Library of Congress Cataloging-in-Publication data
for this title is available from the publisher.

ISBN: 1-58423-013-4
D.L.: M-26101-2001

Printed in Spain

Recipient of the highly coveted Heinrich-Tessenow Gold Medal for architecture in 1998, in addition to several other international prizes, Juan Navarro Baldeweg is one of the most highly acclaimed avant-garde architects and multi-faceted artists living today.

Painter and artist – winner of the Spanish Plastic Arts Award in 1990 – researcher at MIT, Cambridge, MA, member of the Spanish Royal Academy of Fine Arts, professor of design at the Madrid School of Architecture, guest lecturer at Harvard and other major universities, Navarro Baldeweg has much to say to artists and architects alike.

This book was specifically designed to reflect the many sides of his character. In the introductory essay, *A Resonance Chamber*, Navarro Baldeweg reveals his own view of architecture and art in a running discourse. This rigorous text is followed by a section of *Selected Works*, which presents the eighteen designs chosen by Navarro Baldeweg to make up the core of this book in a layout that was carefully planned by the architect in conjunction with the publisher. Next comes a documentary section, *Works and Projects*, which provides a detailed inventory of his output. Under the headings included in this section, reference numbers are given to publications dealing with the building or design in question. The list of publi-cations appears in the comprehensive *Bibliography*, which comes after the key dates for his career and the abbreviated list of awards and competitions that are summed up in the *Biography* section.

With this new volume, Tanais Arquitectura continues to disseminate the consoli-dated work of a contemporary Spanish architect both within Spain and abroad. At the same time as *Navarro Baldeweg* comes out in Spain in the local language, English, German and Italian versions are also being published for the rest of the world.

The publisher would like to thank the Subdirectorate General for Architecture in the Ministry of Development, the Spanish authorities in the area, for their constant encouragement to all those furthering the study and practice of architecture and their moral support in the publication of this book. The readers to whom it is addressed will be able to reap the benefits of this collective effort.

Raul Rispa, Publisher

A Resonance Chamber

Juan Navarro Baldeweg

For Adrián and Víctor

1 *Light and Metals* installation, Vinçon Gallery, Barcelona, 1976

2 Retrospective exhibition at the Valencian Contemporary Art Center, IVAM, 1999

I.

Over the years, both as an architect and as a creator of objects and paintings, I have produced a body of work in which certain motifs can be seen to recur. These themes stem from a need to attest, through my work, to the existence of certain essential dimensions, whether they be components of our physical environment or factors inherent in our own individual, organic nature. These dimensions converge at the very foundations of my oeuvre. My need to attest to them provides not only the inspiration for my work, but also the objectives which have governed its making.

As I see it, this is a thesis that requires us to focus beyond the object as a self-contained, limited, artistic entity, directing our creative gaze rather onto its "exteriority" and thereby situating it in an unlimited continuum. In the process, our underlying aware-ness becomes attuned to a patrimony that is essential, natural and omnipresent.

I like to name these essential dimensions or factors, calling them "light", "gravity", "the horizon" and "the hand". Some of my works reflect this personal categorization, having been made with the express intention of rendering this system of variables explicit and accessible. In some cases the works are deliberately simple, aiming to perform this function for only one of the factors or coordinates, while in others they are more complex and plural, combining several dimensions. Pieces concerned with light, gravity, the horizon and the hand are characterized by their way of isolating one of these categories in their very conception, but I have also made installations and buildings in which they appear in complex amalgam.

With hindsight, I now see the 1976 *Light and Metals* installation at the Vinçon Gallery as a seminal work in which the protagonists of much of my subsequent work can already be identified. In that exhibit, all were brought into play simultaneously. Natural light played a dominant role in the completely white room with a north-facing skylight and two large windows. Gravity was manifest in the motionless, suspended swing. The notion of the horizon occurred experientially as the spectator's view changed with his gradual ascent of the stairs leading to the room, his eye drawn to the weightless swing outlined in the doorway and his gaze then swiveling to left and right between the windows at either end of the visual axis perpendicular to the staircase. The hand was there, too, for the room had been redrawn upon itself in colored lines of blue, green, black, red and yellow. Lines representing the window and its light both imitated reality and were superimposed on it, like the features on a mask, or face-paint which exagger-ates, deforms and enlarges the features beneath.

In any environment, light and gravity impose sensations upon the perceiving subject which he accepts inevitably and passively. The horizon and the hand, however, implicate the subject in action. Visual exploration and action presuppose an organic body which responds with curiosity, moves, engages with his surroundings, and feels motivated by urges to organize, build and shape.

The retrospective exhibition held at the Valencian Contemporary Art Center (IVAM) in 1999 was organized around these notions, physically expressed in two large tables placed in the central space around which paintings and photographs of architecture revolved, as if in thematic orbits, in a way conducive to heterogeneous and interactive sight. This large installation effectively created an imaginary room, a space in which obsessions were assembled and explored, and expanded all the dimensions which had made their seminal appearance in the *Light and Metals* exhibition of 1976.

II.
There are no limited objects, but rather matter and energies entwined in complex knots, extensions of some of whose threads reach our bodies through our senses. They form part of flows of events, and the effects of those flows involve us. Our environment and our presence within it are interdependent, and they flow together to form an integrated whole, engaged in an interactive dynamic. When we consider an object or some part of our environment, we must realize at once that we are actually integral to the process of apprehension, that relationships exist without which its existence would pass undetected.

2

Not all of the infinite number of possible effects exerted by the outside world are phys-ically detected; some are detectable only when amplified, emphatically pointed out or transfigured. Only then do they appear and become obvious, while others pass unnoticed. An external environment touches and transforms another, internal, intra-corporal one, and the signals that reach us via our senses are interiorized within our mental space. Emotion is a response to effects induced during a complex informational process.

Architecture, which can be construed as an interposition along this continuum between two spheres, external and internal, acts as a "box" to enlarge or filter the threads of its uninterrupted, encompassing basic fabric. An image that I always find seductive is that of the room or built space as a resonance chamber, a transformer of foreign signals which translates and adapts them into receptible terms, as imposed by organic nature and culture. In other words, this is a way of understanding architecture as part of nature, an abstract landscape inferred from the natural world and, what is more, directed at establishing an indissolubly powerful alliance with the body as a whole. Its effects are backed up by the memory of countless experiences. Constructed space mobilizes and triggers memories of spontaneous habitation, of the links between space

1

and the body, and of what every culture has made of that relationship. Architecture is a mirror in which we can see an awareness of our physical, organic presence in the world, and this awakens echoes which thrill and stir the emotions. Architecture can be seen as landscape, but also as body art.

We do not, therefore, inhabit a specific piece of architecture so much as a house which is both within and beyond it. A single work of architecture is a concentric, selective interposition, occupying a gap between the all-embracing and the intimate. It stands in both spheres, and reverts to each.

In music, an initial vibration, a wave on the air, is collected and treated, filtered, chan-neled and amplified through a resonance chamber, so that its effects reach our ears as a distinct and differentiated sensation. A sound caused by the wind, when amplified by a bell or metal tube, we hear as a tinkle; the vibration of a string, when qualified by a wooden box, we hear as timbre. What we perceive as sound after sound arranged in time is, in essence, collaboratively produced by the original source of the vibration, the translating instrument and our hearing.

If we say that music is not the instrument, then nor is architecture the box. It is not enough to concentrate our efforts on making the box beautiful. This way of under-standing architecture postulates something more specific: building on the conceptual

2

3

4

5

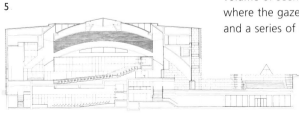

axis which incorporates source and sink, physical origin and sensory destination, and, to extend the metaphor, making a chamber which, when it resonates, creates harmony between both extremes. A piece of architecture imagined as a vehicle, a transitive entity, is conceptually transparent and its mission is to be invisible.

It is my opinion that this interpretation of the ends and means of architecture places a new slant on how architectonic culture should be orientated, its sense of purpose and its role. It calls for a broader focus and a more generous and disinterested approach. I believe that such an approach would immediately contribute to a freer, more agile understanding of how we relate to the made environment.

III.
My first light pieces were created with the aim of constructing and shaping the passage of natural ambient light. The *Five Units of Light* dating from 1974 were already little "resonance chambers" which rendered specific effects of light passing through them clear and perceptible. In their immediacy, they created a typology of effects. One unit consisted of a box incorporating a piece of glass through whose edge one could see how light was enclosed between its surfaces and how it was conducted like an optical fiber. Another unit captured the impression light made on sensitive paper, the shadow and brightness produced by a nearby light bulb creating an elemental, innocent and crude photograph. Inside another box was an area of brightness shining onto paper impregnated with a drop of oil: the bright patch this created was a miniature full moon, making us aware of the flow of light. Another box revealed a luminous interior volume whose upper edges, on the lid, were outlined in black so that it looked like a solid, tangible cube of light. The fifth and last box had a halo – retained as a retinal after-image – around a green square against a blue background, the halo signaling the inseparable link between our visual apparatus and the colors of the external object.

I have had occasion to install in many of my architectural works what amounts to "light pieces" in the approach taken to controlling and channeling the entry of natural light. One example of this sort of "piece" is the rehabilitated interior of Murcia's Segura River Mills Cultural Center, where light travels through the two upper levels occupied by the library to reach the little theater below. A small dome hangs in the air, bordered by an arc of light. Similar intention governs the layout and design of the floating dome structure which roofs the main hall of Salamanca's Convention Center and Exhibition Hall, where the entry of light is used in combination with its suspension in the air to create a weightless, floating effect. Both of these buildings could be described in their entirety as "light boxes" in which natural light is given shape and its presence is celebrated.

After working on these pieces, which featured "shapes" standing out against an un-differentiated "background" of ambient light, I explored structures which made a feature of this uniform, general "background" of homogeneous, indirect north light. Structurally, these architectural models were intentionally designed so that no shadows were cast on their structural components. Porticoes were V-shaped in section, so that vertical light glanced off without creating shadows. I attempted to handle form in such a way that protagonism was limited exclusively to this "background". I avoided all featuring of structural elements in order to make them barely visible. The result was a volume of seemingly palpable, pure, luminous texture, with no figurative obstacles, where the gaze could wander freely. This experimentation gave rise to a set of models and a series of objects halfway between pieces of art and designs of architecture.

In a later period, I again included shapes of direct light in spaces or "backgrounds" of ambient light in much the same way. An example of this can be seen in the 1993 Allende Museum project, where a sun-orientated border of light shines in on a homogeneously lit interior.

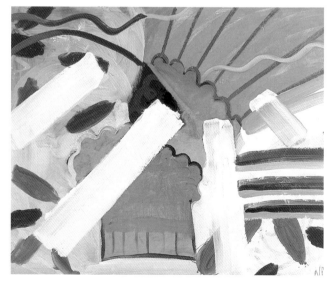

Here, as in other projects, my intention was to create light shapes against backgrounds of general light, introducing warm-toned shapes into an overall environment of colder color. In boxes of uniform light, figurative lights looked like sparks, or like eddies in a stream of water noticeable only when you put in your hand, placing an obstacle into its otherwise imperceptible flow. In other models, the backgrounds became large areas or patches organized as zones of light and shadow. An example of this is the design for the Maritime Museum, part of the Arrecife Marina project for the Canary Island of Lanzarote. There, vertical light and its reflection on the water was used as an ingredient in an engaging visual spectacle.

These designs reproduced situations such as those which occur in any landscape with clouds, rays of sunlight, areas of full sun and shadow, where color varies according to how and where light is orientated and reflected. As experiments, they were cognate with the landscape paintings I was doing at that time. Inspiration and aims were decanted from painting to architecture. Color and light-shapes were both effects created by manipulating light's natural flow. The passage of light and the play of its reverberations were channeled to create shapes and tints in the amorphous stream of energy in which we are immersed.

IV.
Architecture promotes, and stimulates, an awareness of our subjection to the gravitational field. There are architectural situations where matter seems to float and others where evidence of oppressive, weighty materiality is emphasized. Signals of weight or weightlessness appear in very different guises and formal solutions throughout architecture. They refer to the weight of material in such a way that, through empathy, the subject perceives his immersion in the same gravitational field. They trigger in the user or spectator an intimate awareness of the muscular tension that is a necessary response to this permanent and inexorable subjection to gravity.

In a freer and less encumbered way, sculpture, like architecture, is an art in which many designs are based on the meaningful control of weight. Sculpture is used to create an awareness of the distance that exists between any object, its physical constitution and its appearance. This threshold between the apparent and the real provides fertile ground for many works of sculpture. In classical sculpture, the area occupied by the very notion of "pose" overlaps with that occupied by the potential state of balance. Designing a sculpture requires one to define its figures structurally, organizing their elements or component parts in close or distant relation to a gravitational axis, while

1 Retrospective exhibition at the IVAM, 1999

2 Skylight structure. Exhibition area, 1993

3 *Landscape*, oil on canvas, 1991

4 Skylight structure in *Two Orientations*, 1998

4

remaining within the bounds imposed by the stability of the whole. These creative objectives can be seen in modern works of sculpture: Degas' figures of dancers, for example, are real equilibrium pieces; Calder's mobiles are not only equilibrium pieces, but also action pieces that are put in motion by the air, the breeze or the wind; and, more recently, Richard Serra's sculptures rely on weight as an essential ingredient of their stability and arrangement in space.

The swing piece in the *Light and Metals* installation illustrates the effect of suspension in space and in time. Although its gravity-defying pose deceives us, at the same time, echo-like, it makes us aware, through contrast, of a feeling of weight in our own body.

Starting with *Wheel and Weight*, designed in 1974, I made a whole series of pieces based on similar principles, which continue to occupy my interest to this day. They are balanced constructions which aim to surprise, sending warning messages about their equilibrium and inviting questions about their fundamental stability. Many of the pieces place at issue the difference between an apparent instability and an internal structural reality whose equilibrium is undeniable.

The articulation and syntax governing the way in which the structural elements of a building (the capital, the column) are formalized have become full of features which, gratuitous to a greater or lesser degree, can only be explained as demonstrative visual signs of the constructed object's immersion in the gravitational field. In these signs, architecture mirrors the excitement of this immersion. It first informs us and then thrills us physically and psychologically with the realization that all matter shares a common obedience to, and dependency on, natural law.

In many projects, I have treated structures as if they were gravity and light pieces, using both in unison to suggest the experiences of weight and weightlessness: the floating structures used in Murcia and Salamanca, mentioned earlier, are examples of this. A belvedere bridge included in the project presented for the City of Culture in Santiago de Compostela is inspired by gravity pieces. The bridge is supported from a center located outside its curvilinear perimeter, causing the spectator to question the eccentric nature of its support and its equilibrium.

1 *Swing piece*, part of the *Light and Metals* installation, Vinçon Gallery, Barcelona, 1976
2 *Wheel and Weight*, 1974
3 Partial view of the retrospective exhibition at the IVAM, 1999

V.
When we enter a place, our gaze surveys it, looking around for the presence of spatial shapes. It seeks out the limits, the outline of the solids and voids, and it identifies any shape ahead of us as the specific horizon of an enclosed visual area. This enclosure is always located within an external horizon, which encompasses it. The ultimate horizon coincides with that of an optic field, a line which distributes and determines an up and a down, a sky and an earth.

The horizon of a standing man establishes a plane in the air, a surface with singular characteristics that extends throughout space at the level of the organ of sight. As he turns his gaze, a surface hovers at his eye level. His gaze slips and slides freely over it, and defines a ring on which infinite vanishing points occur. The conditions that vision imposes exert a powerful effect, magnetizing and characterizing space. They are a given, a first form which, as soon as there is a subject, contradict any assumption that space is isotropic. Their spontaneous formalization predates all architecture.

This plane is the habitat of the subject's eye, but it is also the place where gazes entwine among people intercommunicating in a group. It is the habitat of exchanged looks – the social eye. As we know, this optical phenomenon provides painting with one of its major themes and expressive resources, put to use in a particularly obvious way in the densely systematized network of subtle interconnections that occurs in classical perspective.

All systems of representation characterize space in terms dictated by the assumed hypotheses of an optical field. As our vision constructs it, space is in itself an inherent, immaterial architecture generated by the mere fact of our bodily presence. In relation to the open horizon, a wall is an interposition which impedes freedom of vision. The gaze slides over and around it or comes up against it and stops. It has veil-like qualities. A designer of architecture must therefore take this power to influence visual routes and direct attention into account. A wall is a shape against a background, and although it is a material fact, its substance is also the stuff of the visual domain.

In addition to their definition as objects, walls, doors and windows possess an optical nature, for part of their being is deduced from the optical field. The notion of the horizon is inherent in any building that stands before us, and freedom of form is by definition the natural concomitant of any building constructed with due regard to visual and luminic flow. The absence of any reference to an encompassing horizon produces feelings of oppression and claustrophobia. Enclosures and horizons are defined on one and the same axis of coordinates and, because of this coincidence, like a cut-out in unlimited space, a piece of

4

4 Belvedere bridge, proposal for the City of Culture in Santiago de Compostela, 1999

5 Detail of the belvedere bridge

5

architecture is possessed of an energy that embraces the entire building like an electric current. It extends to all parts of the work, since they are all engaged in a relationship with an encompassing limit, a wall-less house. Solidarity exists between the built environment and the whole which constitutes its referential background.

The interior of Salamanca's Convention Center and Exhibition Hall is conceived as a porous volume, a complex of concentric areas whose walls the eye can penetrate from any location to obtain glimpses of the external horizon, the space outside. Inherent to this project is a visual fluency which fosters the illusion of the eye's power to give instantaneous shape to the way objects are arranged as it makes its exploratory way to its ultimate goal, the horizon.

The metaphor of the veil and the motifs related to it can help us to interpret the wall as a compact theater stage, where backcloths, curtains and filters may be placed and arranged at will. A wall possesses a substance whose degree of definition can potentially be gradated from opacity to transparency. Contained within its interior, within its section, is a promise of revelation. The quest here is not for the external horizon but for the internal, the intrinsic, landscape. Envisaged thus, the wall becomes an amalgam of concentric skins which, peeled away gradually, leads eventually to an immaterial, diaphanous nucleus. Matter opens up layer by layer, drawing back curtains of different density and transparency. This image explains the decisions that guided the arrangement of the complex "skin" used in Mérida's Regional Government Buildings. It illustrates the significance of the use of materials – their fragmentation and their continuity – such as the purposeful use of granite and Colmenar stone, brick and glass. The same wall metaphor also informs the constructive approach to the outer walls of the building and courtyards of the Villanueva de la Cañada Cultural Center, where layers of wrapping (brick, white gesso, glass) unfold in relation to a continuous wall, as if the interior held the key to the unveiling process.

In the project for a theater in Blois, the enclosure wall was designed to unfold in three layers: red brick, opalescent glass and clear glass. These stacked layers were correlated to the diverse areas of activity which required differing degrees of autonomy and isolation. The auditorium and stage – a place of illusion *par excellence* and, as such, a space that is self-contained, artificial and kept separate from any other reality. The corresponding treatment was an opaque brick band which circumscribed this necessarily segregated and isolated activity. A second enclosure, which confined the previous

1 Convention Center and Exhibition Hall of
   Castilla y León, Salamanca, 1985. Main
   hall and side lobby
2 Presidential Offices and Administrative
   Buildings for the Regional Government of
   Extremadura, Mérida, 1989. Detail of the
   west façade
3 Center for Performing Arts in Blois,
   France, 1991. Model
4 Villanueva de la Cañada Cultural Center,
   1992. North façade

one, contained the stage machinery and supports for artificial lighting which provide the setting for the inner enclosure's virtual reality and make its intimate, artificial on-stage world possible. Opalescent glass walled this enclosure, expressive of what is half seen, a bridge between external reality and internal fiction. A third, ring-shaped enclosure circumscribed these two and was placed above them, crowning the building: inside it contained a relaxation zone made up of a restaurant and a sitting area, with views of both the previous interior enclosures, and of the outside space in the form of the landscape of Blois, the town on the other side of the river. This was expressed physically in the transparency of the upper part of the building, which was made to open onto two realities, one internal and one external. In the Blois project, the building's main activities were matched by the superimposed and vertically unfurled layers of its outer wall. The wall expressed the function of each enclosure and was generated by it.

The relationship between a work of architecture and the horizon was made manifest in the Finnish Pavilion designed by Alvar Aalto for the 1939 New York World Fair. For me, that relationship constitutes the essence of this building. In the pavilion, a large inclined panel or wall, to which our gaze is directed and which displays exhibited material, undulates like a flag. The limits dictated by sightlines seem to have been integrated into this surface, which fluctuates and changes shape to match the exploring gaze. It seems to have been impelled into shape by visual sorties and by the wavering between tension and relaxation that visual negotiation involves. Its division into telescopically superimposed layers reflects the way that the information displayed on them is classified. Its arrangement mirrors a series of horizons corresponding to different visual orbits: near orbits take in nearby objects, the things closest to us, while more distant orbits take in landscapes and distant sights. This diversity is matched by a two-way – horizontal and vertical – display and by the systematic presentation of surfaces to our view. A nation, a land, its people and the products of their labor are presented here in a way as coherent as a system of perspective, but better than that, since this is a multiple system that accommodates dynamism, simultaneity and juxtaposition within it. Here, architecture has reproduced a system which allows images to be juxtaposed in essential relation to the gaze, and built a shape that seems to be a parallel version of our vision and its exploratory habits. Attached to this architectonic framework, impressions such as vignettes of the natural environment and the life of its people have been arranged in a purely visual itinerary.

19

VI.

The hand permits the clearest expression of responses which originate in an intimate, organic world. Drawing exposes the whole body, but the products of manual processes used in the trades and crafts, and even machine-made objects, are also impregnated with an empathy-triggering organic element. The hand is concealed to a greater or lesser degree in all constructed things, and we discern its faint imprint in anything that has been shaped. The body and a spiritual sort of memory coexist, tightly intertwined, in our urge to shape.

A scribble is the mark that this urge produces when it seeks unlimited expression, and it reflects something that we recognize immediately as profoundly human. These automatic marks, whose dance condenses a huge array of experiences, are a gratuitous manifestation of the productive urge, free of utilitarian purpose. The hand is a sort of frontier where a tangle of strokes, expressive of perceptual deposits and recollections

1

2

of a boundless agglomeration of basic units of action, waits to leap out, helter skelter. Image and action condense into one, for movement is basic to drawing and any figurative interpretation brings a program of interlinked actions into play. Drawing is a process in time: it is a succession of acts. The hand pursues an inexhaustible repertoire of shapes and actions, supplied both from a shapeless, disorganized fund of juxtaposed images, and from a random, irresolute moving force. Likenesses and gestures, representations of figures and even embryonic movements, emerge simultaneously through the hand. In addition to these images, and closely allied to them, signs emerge suggestive of such actions as bending, folding, plaiting, punctuating, underlining, accentuating: signs representing rhythmic and sensual perceptions – namely, touch – and shifts from stillness to action – the continuous and the intermittent, the sluggish and the quick, the brutal and the delicate – expressed in pattern. There is a decisive hand and a tentative one, a sword-wielding hand and a fan-wielding one. In all constructed objects we like to detect a hand print through which these remote experiences "reverberate" and reveal themselves. We like to detect its imprint and to sense its closeness, however overshadowed or hidden it may be. Its presence impregnates all constructed things, imposing a deliberate, intentional and direct approach almost without our realizing it. It endows buildings with the precise scale that stems from the organism and extends to other organic bodies that are not the human body.

The free-hand drawing of the *Light and Metals* room was done in the room itself, like a superimposed structure. Its lines, which reflected the very reality on which they were being drawn, constituted an expressive image of an urge to dominate, a never fully satisfied territorial urge: an example of the body resounding in the incorporeal, like a voice echoed back by woodlands, rocks or mountains. Much of the motivation for what I call "hand pieces" derives from the intuited need to define a category of gratuitous forms – a category of forms that do not obey purely constructive laws. These pieces stem from the desire to segregate, to liberate demands that pull a design in opposite directions, and ensure coexistence between the inorganic and the organic, the intimate and the remote, the expressive and the spontaneous.

The pieces exhibited on one of the large tables in the IVAM retrospective exhibition were similarly motivated. I made automatic drawings or pieces of calligraphy in the air, drawn structures standing in space which, by this process, became a territory dominated by objectless graffiti. The redrawn window in the *Light and Metals* exhibition was an early expression of the same intention, replicating reality on top of reality itself, like a mask over a face. Later came spirals or whirlwinds of energy made visible, like the energy vortices or birds in flight used in the installation at the 1996 Milan Triennial. The "scribbles" in the recent IVAM exhibition were inspired by the hand's spontaneous impulses and were intended to constitute a separate and independent layer within another construction. The figurative magic of the architecture of Alvar Aalto or the work of Frank Gehry, for example, emanates from their manual transparency, from the fact that the shapes they create obey primordial urges, from the clearly whimsical manual origin we detect in them. In these cases, and in many others, their forms are indissoluble hybrids which condense both constructional and functional demands and a manual approach, however remote and gratuitous. As in calligraphy, a dual plane of reference is in operation: conventional signaling and specific physical expression. Calligraphy and its flourishes occupy a space between two extremes. At one extreme, it serves as vehicle for propositional content, as the referent for a word or phrase, and at the other, for the execution of a manual creation and bodily gesture. In these pieces, manual motivations float, obligation-free, with a life of their own. The "hand pieces" are autonomous constructions which demand nothing for themselves and differ from other things which have been constructed to meet the usual requirements imposed by functional or structural order.

VII.

Like any other object, a work of architecture exists on the surface, but it is the fruit on a plant whose roots are few but whose catchment is vast. The effects of a building are multiplied when it is inhabited, for a house is permeable both outwards, towards the natural exterior, and inwards, towards the intimate and organic interior. The aim of an architectural project is consciously to provide a setting which will serve as a vehicle for certain essential variables so that they become an integral, discernible part of our lives. An architectural design is a design for a simple, clean box, which allows certain radical components freedom of movement. A building incorporates a gamut of dimensions, and a room expresses a special message emitted by an energy field, called up by resonance and transmitted into the realm of our experience.

1 Model, research project at MIT, Cambridge, MA, 1977

2 *Night*, spatial structure drawing, 1998

Selected Works

House of Rain Single Family Residence

Alto de la Hermosa. Santander. Spain
1978

1

1 Sketch
2 Area map
3 View from the road

2

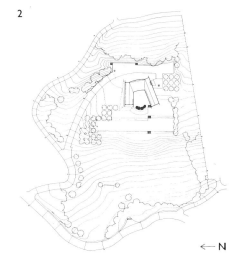

← N

The design centered on the construction of a single-family house on the top part of a plot of land dominating a valley. On this site, the house was oriented towards the west, following the slope of the ground and the views of the valley.

The mass of the building was laid out in a "U" shape ground plan, consisting of two advancing arms linked by a curved volume, in which the program was developed on a single floor. The living area, which opens and extends into a patio-garden that functions as an open-air room, was situated in one of the wings. Its low silhouette, with double-sloping roofs, identifies it with the traditional constructions of isolated country houses. The house was set on level ground, on an artificial horizontal plane created through cut and fill. The advance of the two arms across this horizontal plane is illustrative of the intervention on the slope, with its directional inflection towards the valley.

In the profile of the house, the pergola delimiting the garden and interior patio stands out. Its height reaches the upper vertex of the gables, uniting its figure with that of the overall volume of the house, and defining an imaginary space that extends beyond the patio.

The construction of the entire work is structured fundamentally by three horizontal layers or strata, defined and differentiated by the qualities of their materials: elements finished in stone at the base, above this a glassed area, and finally, a traditional roof of zinc.

The main entrance or portal to the house is found, after a circuitous route from the access road, in the curved central wall of the convex volume. The door is set in a blind wall, in a vacuum of sensations which conditions one's appreciation, by contrast, of the visual richness revealed on opening the door. The gaze appropriates the interior, and escapes towards the patio through the door opposite the entry, losing itself beyond in the valley, in a vista framed by the pergola. This axis structures the plan of the house and its insertion in the terrain.

1 Rain House, sketch dating from 1979
2 General elevation
3 Ground plan

1

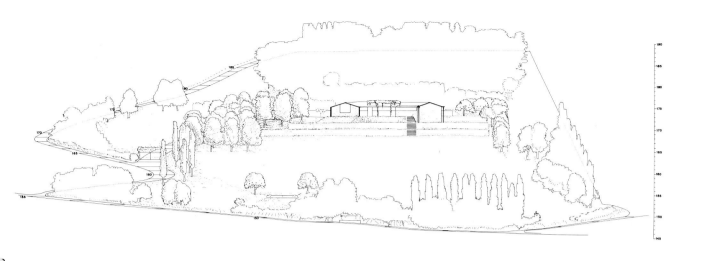

2

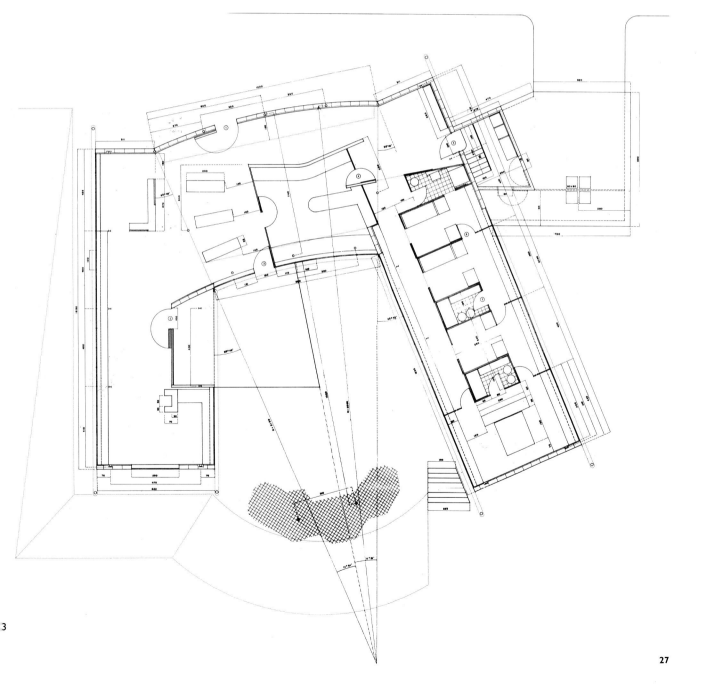

3

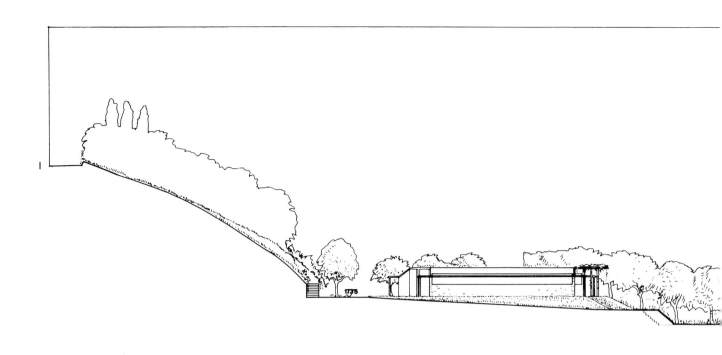

2

1 Longitudinal section
2 Partial view from the north

Rehabilitation of the Segura River Mills for a Hydraulics Museum and Cultural Center

Murcia. Spain
1984-1988

The old bridge, the walls that contain the river around the bridge, and the old mills of the city form a unique urban nucleus that characterizes the heart of Murcia and forms the most significant point of encounter between the city and the Segura River. The great impact that the rehabilitation of the mills was to have on the overall image of the capital was evident.

The mills, together with the containing walls and the old stone bridge, were conceived according to plans drawn up by Jaime Bort. Construction of the whole complex was carried out between 1718 and 1741. The initial plan for this part of the neighborhood of El Carmen was a product of the same impulse of reform and development promoted in the 18th century by the Spanish Count of Floridablanca.

At one time, the mills consisted of a prismatic construction parallel to the river, with an open canal behind it, in line with the containing wall. Its flat roof was level with and connected to the raised level of the city above the river's walls. This rectangular element housed the line of hydraulic mechanisms of the mills on a single floor. Its strong and sober construction was ennobled on its upper part by an order of pilasters, indicating the level of the work spaces in its interior. This original unitary condition was taken into consideration in preparing the mills' return to public use as a Museum of Hydraulics and Cultural Center. Decisions made during the design of the rehabilitation project gave preference to a return to the most genuine original appearance of the mills.

31

The plans for the new Museum and Cultural Center reveal the way in which the continuous and linear scheme of the former mills coexists with the formation of spaces which tend to emancipate and organize themselves as autonomous places. The auditorium on the lower floor and the library above it are arranged around a vertical axis which coincides with a skylight well that illuminates the reading rooms and conducts light to the center of the auditorium. The coexistence of a linear spatial fluidity and the creation of a nucleus of individual compositional elements can be easily appreciated in the sections and in the general profile of the elevations. In the portion rising from the level of the upper walk, the closed, sculptural volume of the library can be clearly distinguished, as can that of the cafeteria-restaurant, which opens in a stepped form towards the walkway, creating a place appropriate for outdoor use.

The composition and ordering of the openings in the elevations, as much on the north as on the south, also testify to the reconciliation between the linearity of the complex and the formation of nuclei around the main activities. On the north elevation, the regular rhythm of the openings corresponding to the water exits on the lowest part of the mills coincides with that of the openings between the pilasters on the upper section. On the southern elevation, that of the lower level of the mills, the main foci of the three-dimensional internal

1

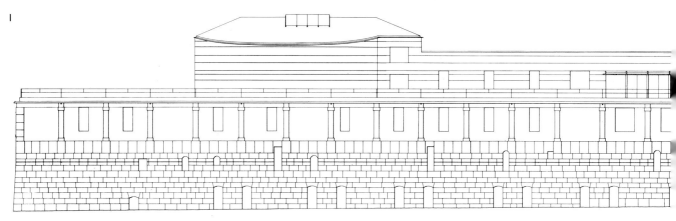

0 1m   5m

2
3

organization are equally legible in the composition of the windows and entry. The plan of the entry reveals the intersection of routes descending to the plaza. The access doors are visible from the ramps and give a sense of focus to the descent.

The southern side of the plaza is enclosed on the west by the former stables, whose rehabilitation as a temporary exhibition hall complements the program of the Museum.

The criteria for the rehabilitation were oriented in opposite directions: while the design sought to implement a rigorous restoration of the original order of the mills, it also proposed the free construction of an addition which, without altering this basic image, made better use of the Center.

Both criteria – rigor and freedom – supported the generation of urban life that the Museum and Center, in their form and use, could provoke. The proposal thus took place on two levels. The basic historic stratum or sediment, the same stratum that supports the rest of the city's architecture, was restored, while the addition above hosted a new formal and constructive variety, in accordance with the new uses. Consequently, the rehabilitation, though in part purist, did not deny the accumulative logic behind the spontaneous additions made to the mills beginning in the 19th century. The project demonstrates that the relation between the historical or traditional and the actual or present can be made visible in a stratified form.

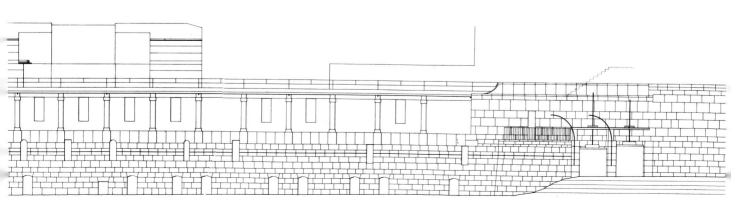

1 First floor plan
2 Ground floor plan
3 Cafeteria interior
4 View of the terrace from the cafeteria

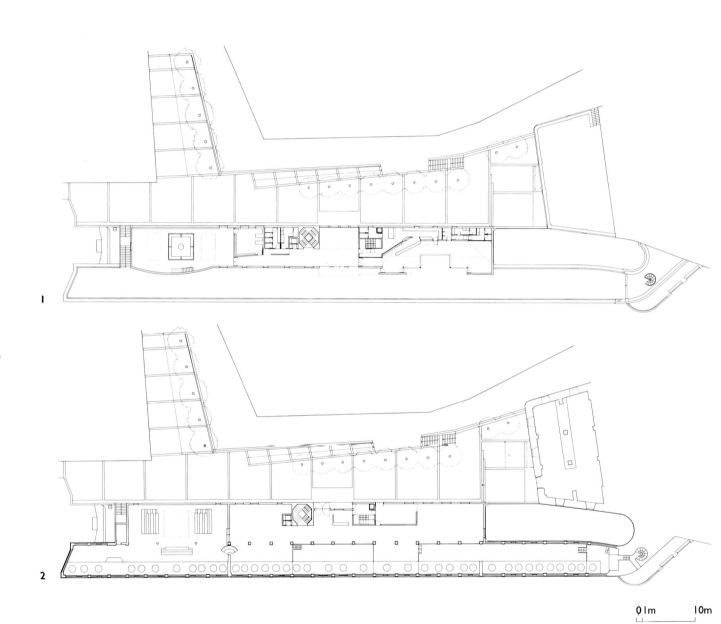

1

2

0 1m   10m

3

4

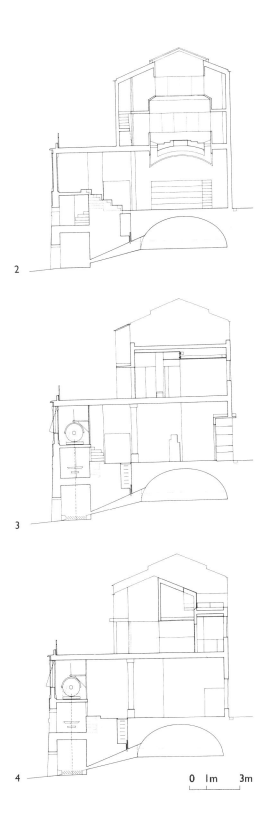

2

3

4

0 1m   3m

1 Reception area
2 Section through the library
3 Section through the entries
4 Section through the cafeteria and
  the museum

DEVELOPER Spanish Ministry of Public Works
STRUCTURAL CALCULATIONS Julio Martínez Calzón
CONSTRUCTION COMPANY Cubiertas y MZOV, S.A.

Castilla y León Convention Center and Exhibition Hall

Salamanca. Spain
1985-1992

Architecture's sphere of operation is the physical world, its mission the definition of objects, the construction of material elements. However, the peculiarity of the architecture of this Convention Center lies in its attention to a complementary context – a context that reveals itself through concrete objects and figures.

In the Center, and especially in its interior, architecture reflects the protagonism of the basic coordinates of light, gravity, or space suggested by a horizon opening in a concentric progression. The cupola covering the main hall is activated as an experience in natural lighting, oscillating between an appearance of weight and one of weightlessness. This cupola allows the gaze to follow, beyond it, its own implicit geometry, which extends to a greater limit that also embraces the lobbies, stage and perimeter spaces. There is, then, a transcendence of appearances, and what comes to the foreground plane is the limited experience of the background: the light, the gravity, the horizon. This was one of the objectives pursued in the conception of the building.

The Vaguada de la Palma river bed is the natural topographic limit of the historic quarter of Salamanca, a boundary reaffirmed on the Centre's site by the containing wall built with materials from the old Roman walls. The location of the plot on the perimeter of the walled precinct, and the appearance of this wall as a pedestal, inspired the image of the future Center. In this

cultural landscape, the intervention reinforced the site's character as a plinth; hence the modelling of the Center in such a way as to recompose and reaffirm the simple volumetric impression of the wall.

While the building was understood as a projection of the constructed mass of the city on this base, at the same time it conserved the character of a physical limit, in which an access path was opened and a threshold created in the manner of a *propylaeum*. The new building was endowed with a triple characterization: as a base to the old city, as a wall construction whose profile clearly stood out in the lower perimeter of the city, and as a connecting lobby between the consolidated upper urban core and the Vaguada park.

The complex surrounding this connecting passage draws into play the significant experience of three constructive archetypes: an architecture of walls or boxes, an architecture of lintels, and a cupola that is seen through the arches that penetrate the center.

The program was resolved in two visible volumes, used to frame the intermediate plaza and joined at lower floor level. The larger volume was designed to house the auditoriums, while the smaller volume was made to rise from the sculpted mass of the open-air auditorium. The interior space of the principal volume was conceived as architecture inside architecture. The main hall was equipped with 1300 seats, and the small hall with 460.

1 Sketch

2 Exterior view

Pages 40-41, Main entry to the convention area

Even though the halls are independent, a single spatial identity was achieved between them through the double-height spaces of their side vestibules. The intention was to solve the complex problem with a single gesture. The architecture was generated both in continuity and in rupture, in free plan and in differentiated spaces. A cupola floats over the main auditorium. The geometry of its stepped inside face guarantees its acoustic performance. Its form follows the outline of an encompassing spherical cupola that extends across the entire building, visible as much in the interior as in the design of the exterior walls.
The building was conceived as a single whole from its constructive genesis. The perception of the structure was animated by the treatment of natural light. The sky light sketches the essential constituents of the internal space, constructing it, conducting views towards the vertical openings and illuminating the walls over which it cascades.

The cupola was suspended from the pairs of load bearing walls, which also act as beams that conduct the loads, through their arched forms, to the edges of the building perimeter. The concentration of the loads on these vertices made it possible to create an architecture free of columns in the space of the main auditorium, stage and lobbies, thereby warranting the encompassing continuity of the ceiling. The fact that the internal arches belong to the sphere outlined by the cupola means that there is no break in the spatial and geometric unity. The cupola over the principal auditorium, suspended in the air and silhouetted by the light, is seen in a balanced tension between weight and weightlessness. The ceiling thus appears to float in the air.
Finally, the materials, colors and scales of the building were purposefully chosen with a view to integrating the new building into the urban landscape.

1

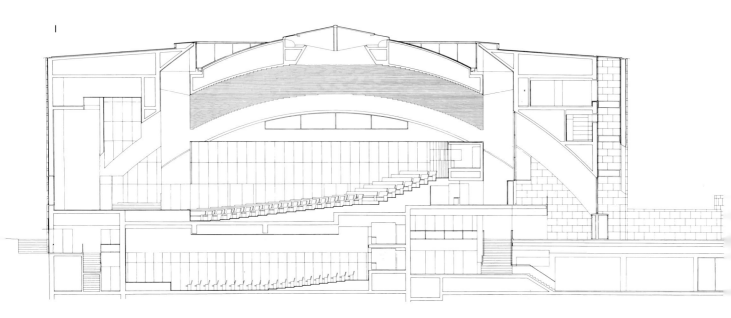

2

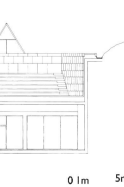

0 1m   5m

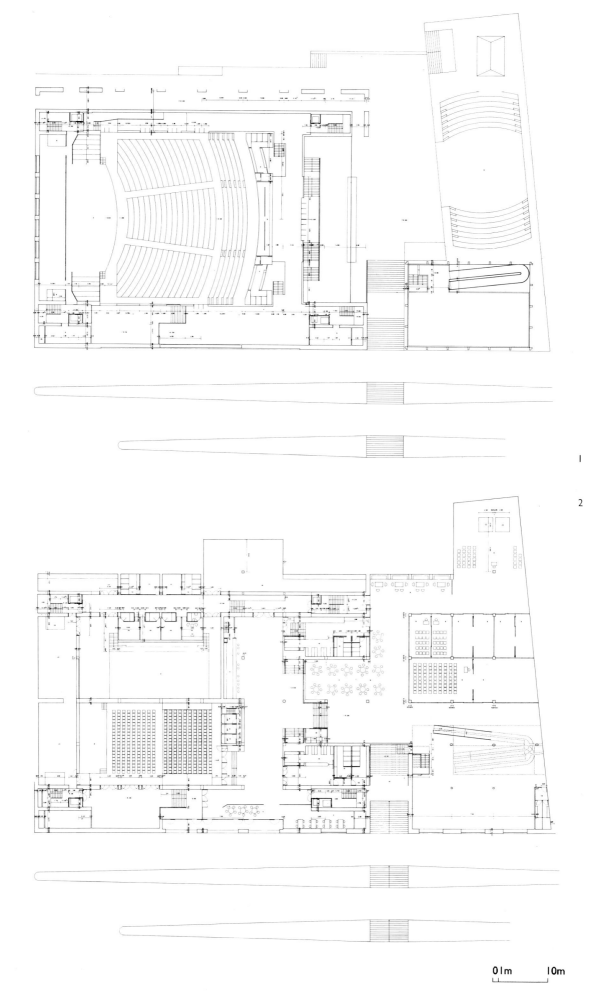

1

2

0 1m   10m

1 Floor plan, levels +3.00, +3.50
2 Floor plan, levels -3.50, -5.20
3 Main hall and side lobbies

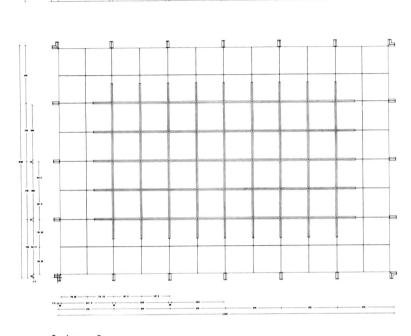

1 Exhibition hall roof: section, plan, and details

2 Ramp to the exhibition halls

0 1m   3m

1

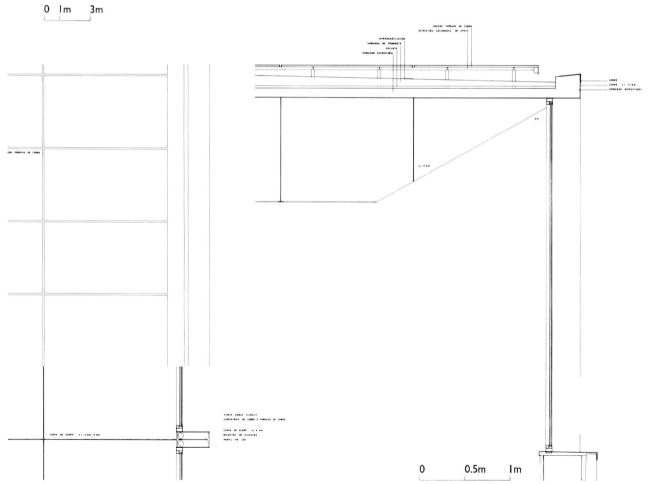

0   0.5m   1m

2

DEVELOPER Castilla y León Convention Center and Exhibition Hall Trust
STRUCTURAL CALCULATIONS Julio Martínez Calzón
CONSTRUCTION COMPANY Teconsa, Tecnología de la Construcción, S.A.

Pedro Salinas Public Library and Social Services Center

Madrid. Spain
1982-1989 and 1990-1994

The program for the Social Services Center was distributed between two buildings on the elevated plaza that dominates the Puerta de Toledo arch and traffic circle. The arrangement of the buildings in an enfolding gesture created a rectangular open-air space, which is reached via a stair-ramp from the Puerta de Toledo circle, as well as from the pedestrian walkway that is a continuation of Paloma Street. This enfolding layout and the modeling of the ground reflect the original topography of the site, in which the plaza platform was left untouched by the excavations carried out in another intervention undertaken to open up Gran Vía de San Francisco Avenue.

The masses of these buildings reflect to a large degree the great care taken over their scale and presence in the Puerta de Toledo Circle. The balance of volumes and the play of solids and voids fall within a conceptual ring or envelope of little height that encircles the Circle's triumphal arch, towards which it is oriented, at the limits of the most appropriate scale. The void of the upper plaza establishes a complementary dialogue with the solid drum of the library's cupola on the other side of Toledo Street.

The program of the second wing of the Social Services Center is similar to that of a day care center, including social group services such as a dining hall and a laundry room, workshops and classrooms. The building also features a multi-purpose hall specially designed to host dance classes and theraupeutic gym sessions.

The child care center stands as a prolongation of the Virgen de la Paloma Church, describing an arc that shapes the pedestrian street connecting Paloma Street with the new elevated plaza over the Puerta de Toledo circle.

In the library, the newly established ground level acquires importance in

1 General floor plan
2 General elevation
3 View of the Social Services Center from the Puerta de Toledo arch

1

N

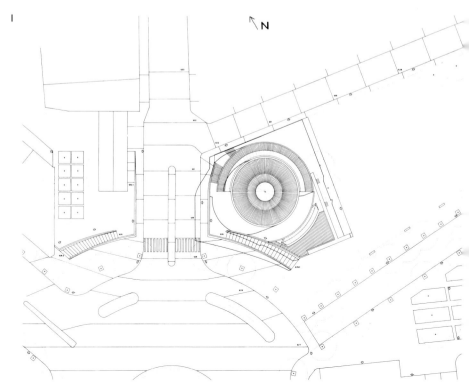

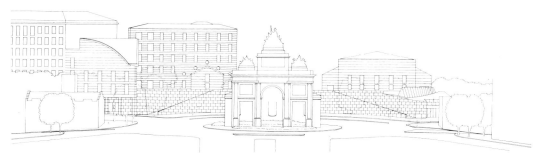

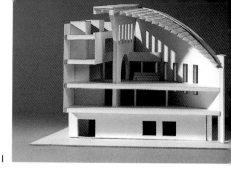

1

2

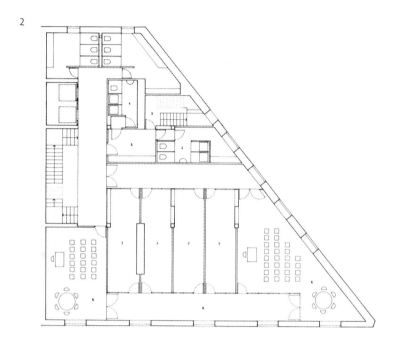

3

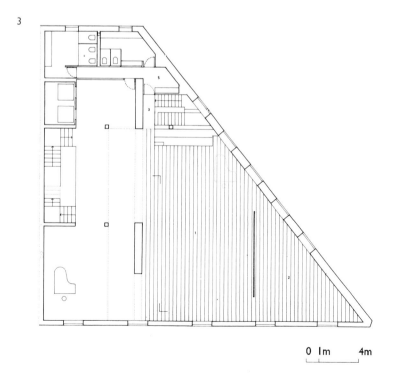

0 1m   4m

the definition of the back of the
Puerta de Toledo circle and the
mouth of Toledo Street. The level
of the plaza in front of the church
is maintained almost at the same
elevation, following its natural slope
until it reaches the circle, which it
approaches at the height of a look-
out and onto which it descends
through a ramp. The break in level
that occurred during the development of the second section of Gran
Vía de San Francisco Avenue is thus
left visible.
The containing wall and ramp
between the elevated plaza and the
traffic circle have their symmetrical
response on the other side of Toledo
Street, in the base of the public
library.
The tension that arises from the
simultaneous effects of concavity and
convexity is essential to the spatial
experience of the circle. The richness
of intentions for these elements is
the same as in the competition
proposal of 1982.
The design for the library integrates
three constructive considerations: the
modeling of the ground plane; the
determination of the form according
to external considerations and, simultaneously, through an identification
with the archetype of the cupola
drum; and, finally, the internal distribution and arrangement of the
program, which is tributary to these
formal considerations.
The library stands out on the plaza as
a building of civic character, with a
clearly sketched profile that concedes
to the urban space the volume that
the place requires. The building has
four floors, which house the different
functions of a district library's general

4

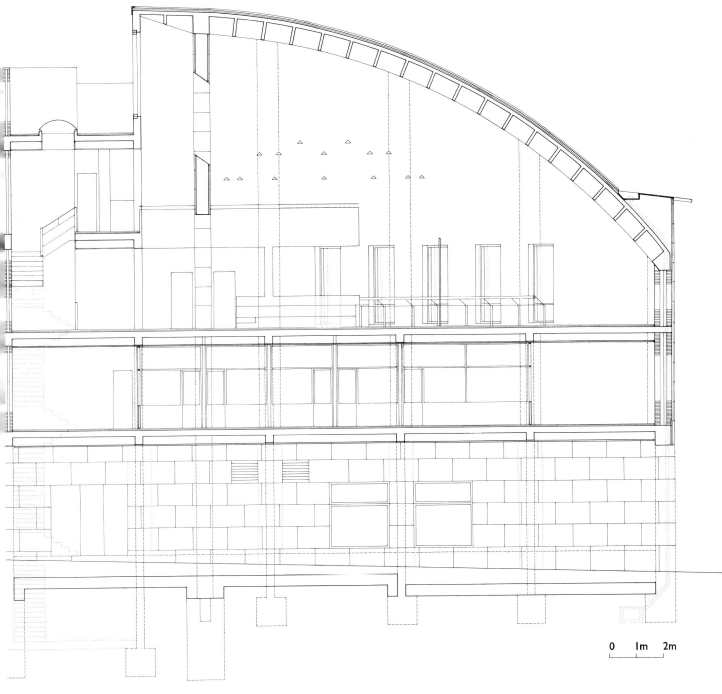

5

0   1m   2m

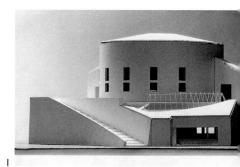

1

program. The children's library, which is housed on the lower floor, has been endowed with an independent side entrance. This lower floor also includes a general book deposit for the entire library of some 160 square meters and a mechanical services room with an entry from the side street.

The street level contains a lending library of 44,000 volumes in radially-arranged book stacks which are easily accessed and controlled. The auditorium, with a capacity of 70, is found on this same floor. Stairs and an elevator on this level rise to the reading room on the upper floors. The reading room includes an independent access from the Puerta de Toledo circle via the stair-ramp. It is arranged on two floors, with a double-height area in which the bookcases are arranged in stepped levels, and contains 156 seats for readers and a shelf capacity of 10,000 volumes. An audiovisual area completes the program on this second level, with a capacity of 14 audio stations and 18 video stations. A magazine area has also been foreseen, with seating for 20 readers.

The structural design and natural light effects inside the cupola's drum were the object of special detailed consideration.

On the outside, the base of the library was finished in gray granite and the upper walls in natural white stone. In the design of these surfaces, the joints of the stone, the composition of the openings, and the treatment of the roofs – the necessary conjunction with the buildings of the Social Services Center – were always taken into account.

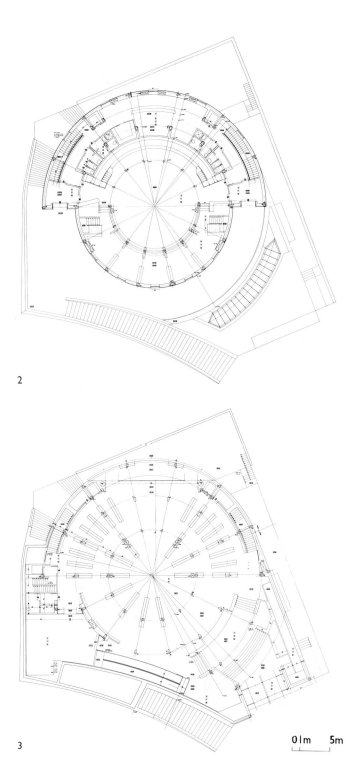

2

3

0 1m   5m

4

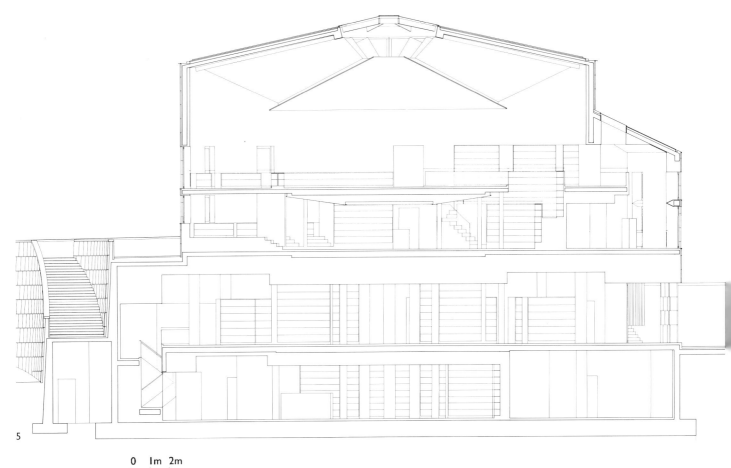

5

0 1m 2m

DEVELOPER Autonomous Community of Madrid
STRUCTURAL CALCULATIONS Julio Martínez Calzón
CONSTRUCTION COMPANY Fersa, Orive, S.A.

1

1 Reading room interior
2 View of the Pedro Salinas Library from the
  Puerta de Toledo arch

2

56

Regional Government of Extremadura
Presidential Offices and Four Administrative Buildings

Mérida. Spain
1989-1995

The site inspired a building of great formal simplicity whose image fits naturally between the nucleus formed by the historic Alcazaba fortress and the Roman bridge, on the one hand, and the plaza located at the end of the modern bridge built by Santiago Calatrava, on the other. This image was intentionally designed to connect the two nuclei and to create, with them, a vital whole. The abstract and linear appearance of the new complex provides a necessary measure of ambiguity between the two concrete figures of the urban enclaves located at its extremes. Between them, the building dominates a large portion of the city's skyline as seen from the other side of the Guadiana River, forming part of a distant horizon. Hence the need for a stark, clear image that could stand out from a distance.

The three glazed terraces or voids cut into the prismatic solid serve as a visible partition between the administrative departments and highlight the sense of frontality of the façade. The openings on the upper floors are grouped around these three concavities. The rest of the upper wall, which is blind, reaffirms the building's formal purity. Its volumetric definition harmonizes with the simple forms of the Alcazaba. By acting as an extension of the fortress, with which it forms a unified whole, the building creates a grand urban façade along the river's edge.

Special attention was given to the building's contact with the ground. The discovery on the site, during the execution of the project, of valuable remains from the Roman era led to a reconsideration of the initial structure of the ensemble, which was substituted for another that could "bridge" the

1 Sketch
2 Area Map
3 View from the Alcazaba fortress

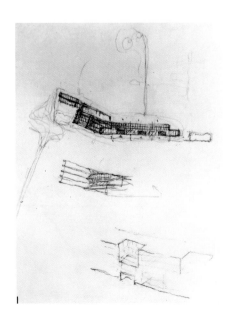

2

N

3

excavation site. The building was thus made to coexist with the archeological deposit. In structural terms, this required a reduced number of supports. From the point of view of creating a dialogue with the ruins, the building follows and reinforces the more general aspects of the site – those which stand out for their urban or geographic character, such as the wall or the Roman road which crosses part of the site. The building thus reproduces the larger outline of the wall and the preexisting urban border, on the one hand, and

protects the ruins, on the other, acting as a neutral frame for the smaller constructive particulars found in the interior of the excavations.

On the ground level, zones of archeological reserve were created. Patios were also opened and aligned parallel to the Roman road in order to illuminate the ground floor and shed light over the archeological remains. In this way, the form of the administration building, which responds to the impulse that emerges from the ground, appears to float freely over the site.

1 West elevation
2 General floor plan
3 Floor plan, level +8.90
4 Floor plan, level +1.70, +3.50
5 Partial view of the west façade

1

2

3

4

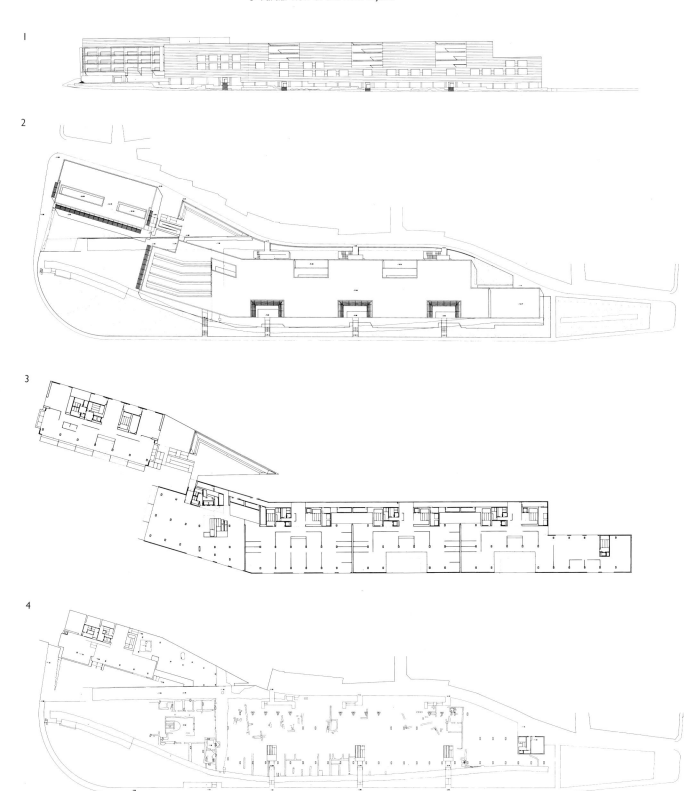

0 1m   20m

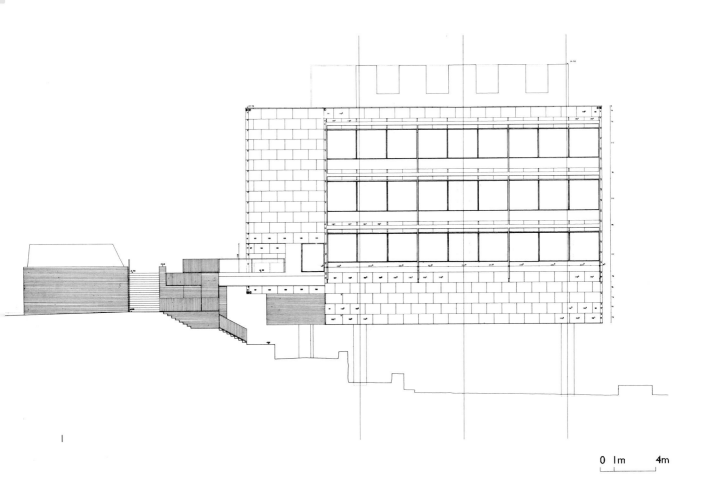

1

0 1m   4m

2

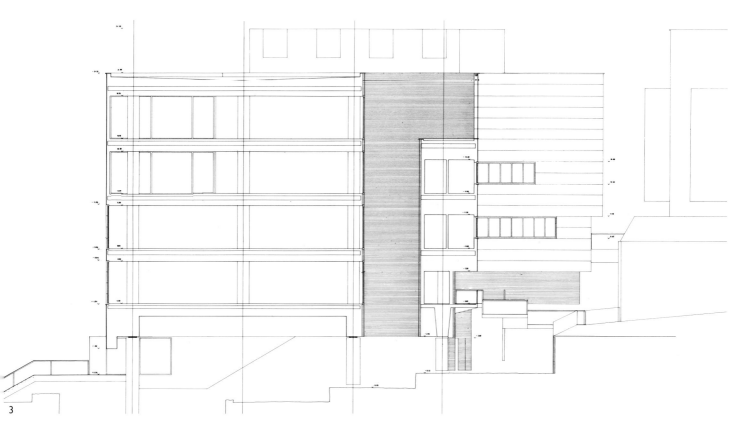

3

1 North elevation of Administrative Building D

2 Partial view of Administrative Building D and Presidential Offices

3 Cross section through the patio of Administrative Building C

4 Archeological remains

4

1 Elevation and plan of *brise-soleil* detail
2 Section of *brise-soleil* detail
3 Partial view of *brise-soleil*

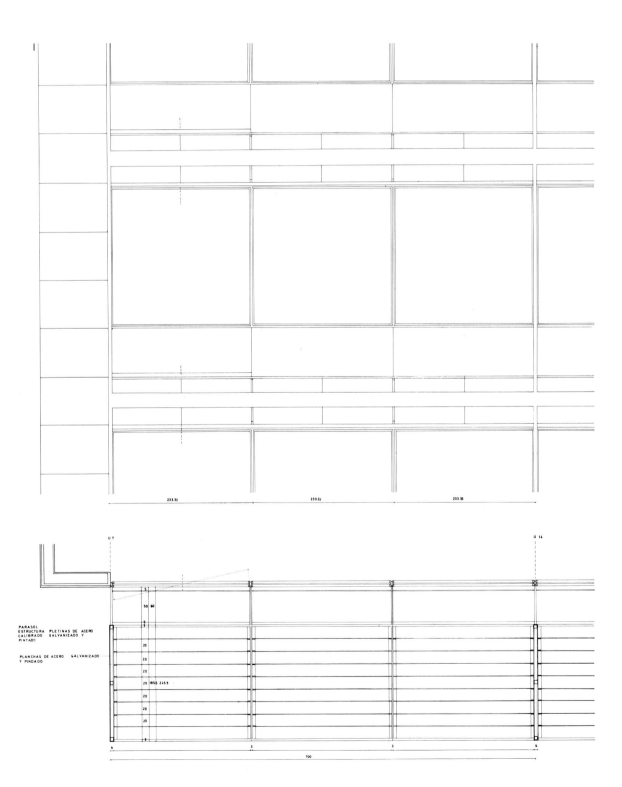

2

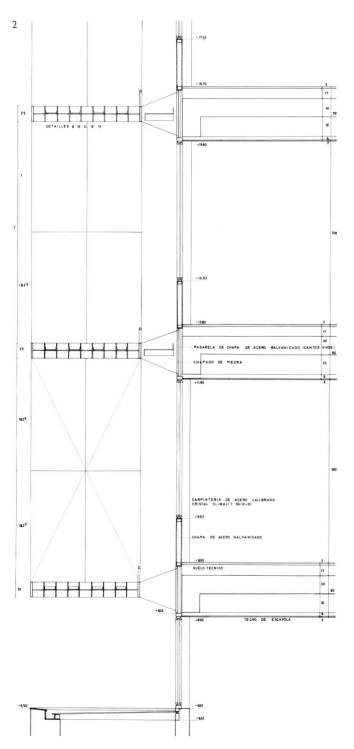

DETALLES 9 10 11 12 13

+17.42

+16.70

+15.80

PASARELA DE CHAPA DE ACERO GALVANIZADO (CANTOS VIVOS)

CHAPADO DE PIEDRA

+13.52

+12.80

+11.90

CARPINTERIA DE ACERO CALIBRADO
CRISTAL CLIMALIT 10+12+10

+9.62

CHAPA DE ACERO GALVANIZADO

+8.90

SUELO TECNICO

+8.06

+8.00   TECHO DE ESCAYOLA

+6.50   +6.50

+6.32

3

DEVELOPER Regional Government of Extremadura
STRUCTURAL CALCULATIONS Julio Martínez Calzón, Juan
Francisco de la Torre
CONSTRUCTION COMPANY Ferrovial, S.A.

Mahón New Courthouse

Mahón. Minorca. Spain
1992-1996

Despite its small size, this new courthouse plays a decisive role in the urban conception and master plan of the surrounding area. In its public character, it is the dominant element of a new internal urban space, equipped with gardens and sports facilities, and bordered by a new road that prolongs the streets of San Manuel and Madrid, in the neighborhood of Santa Eulalia.

The design included the entire building site on which, in addition to the courthouse, it created a parking area behind the building and an entry for police vehicles. The landscaped parking area is defined by stucco walls designed in keeping with local building customs.

The courthouse was constructed in large part with traditional methods of masonry building and white stucco finishing, thus identifying its image with the urban context in which the building is located.

Despite the small scale and the standardized appearance of the constructed volume, the building was endowed with a public character through the design of the entry and the double-height order of the upper floors on the façade looking out over the new street (San Manuel – Madrid). Here, the aluminum screen, finished in a warm gray color, resembles the screens and filters of light and views of residential urban architecture, from which it is distanced by differences in scale and color.

The program was developed in four levels. On the ground floor are the civil registry, a hearing room, a private office for lawyers and procurers, a forensics room, waiting rooms, and restrooms.

The first floor contains a second hearing room, a judge's private office, penal and prosecutor's offices, a secretarial office and a civil office, as well as employees' restrooms.

The second floor includes another judge's private office, a penal and civil office, a secretarial office, and the archives.

Finally, on the lower floor, corresponding to the basement of the building, are located two holding cells, a suspect line-up room, a room for the police, an inactive archive for the civil registry, a courthouse archive, an evidence storage room, and a room for mechanical services.

1 Sketch
2 Main entry

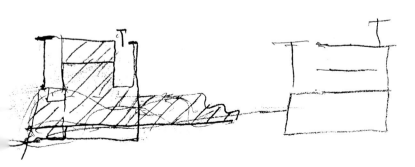
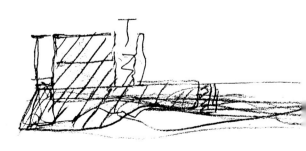

1 Roof plan

2 Floor plan, level 0.00

3 Detail of the staircase

Pages 72-73, East façade

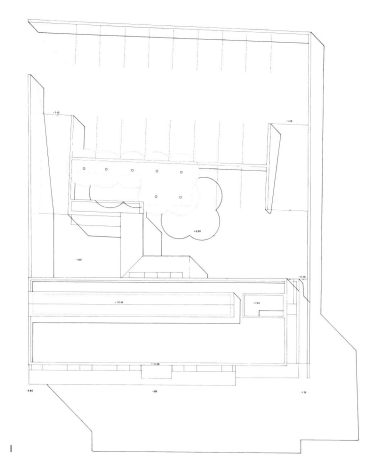

1

2

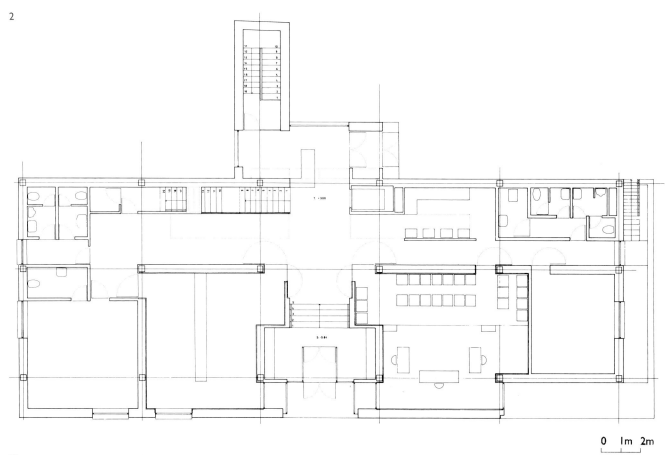

0 1m 2m

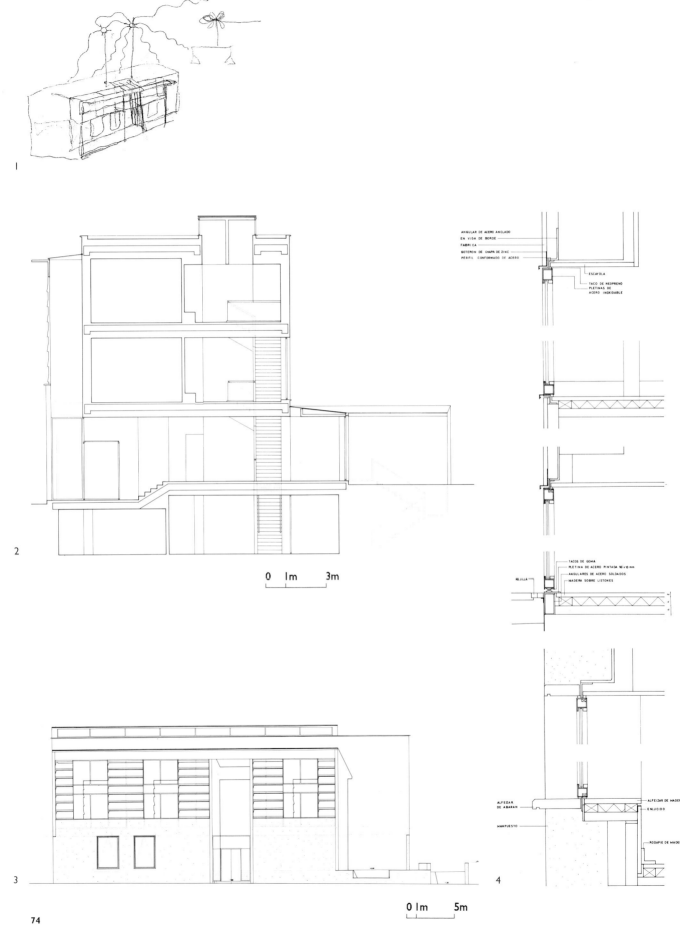

ANGULAR DE ACERO ANCLADO
EN VIGA DE BORDE
FABRICA
GOTERON DE CHAPA DE ZINC
PERFIL CONFORMADO DE ACERO

ESCAYOLA
TACO DE NEOPRENO
PLETINAS DE
ACERO INOXIDABLE

TACOS DE GOMA
PLETINA DE ACERO PINTADA 50 x 10 mm
ANGULARES DE ACERO SOLDADOS
MADERA SOBRE LISTONES

REJILLA

ALFEIZAR
DE ABARAN

MAMPUESTO

ALFEIZAR DE MADERA
ENLUCIDO

RODAPIE DE MADERA

0 1m   3m

0 1m   5m

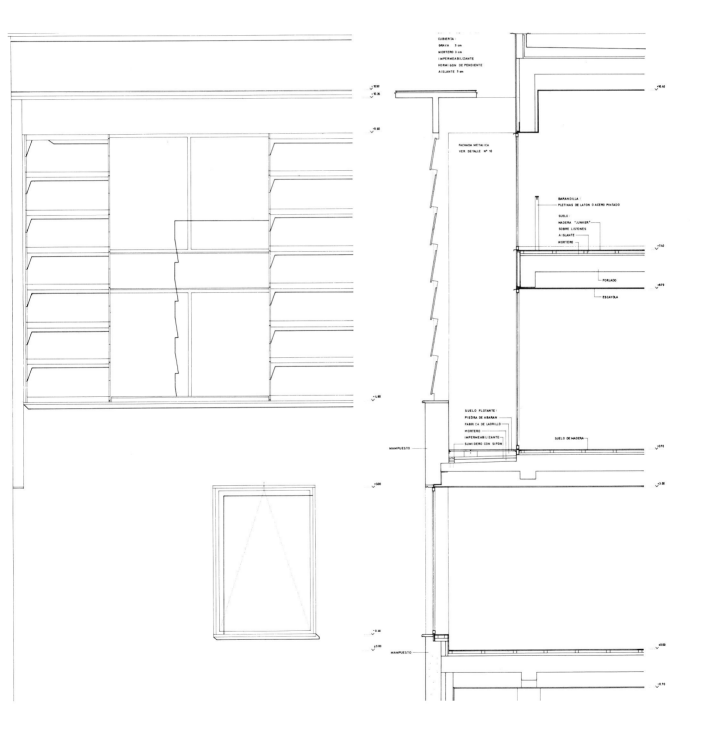

1 Elevation, plan, and section of entry metal-work detail

2 Partial view of the entry

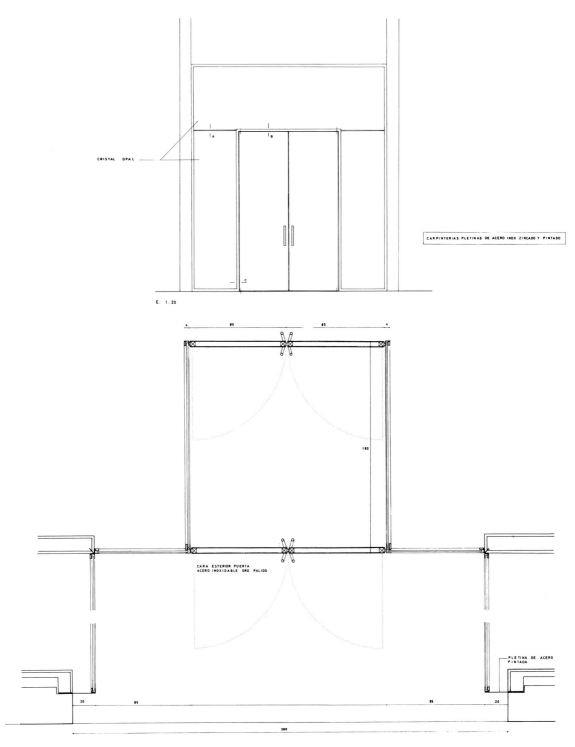

CRISTAL OPAL

CARPINTERIAS·PLETINAS DE ACERO INOX. ZINCADO Y PINTADO

E. 1:20

CARA ESTERIOR PUERTA
ACERO INOXIDABLE ORO PALIDO

PLETINA DE ACERO
PINTADA

0   1m   3m

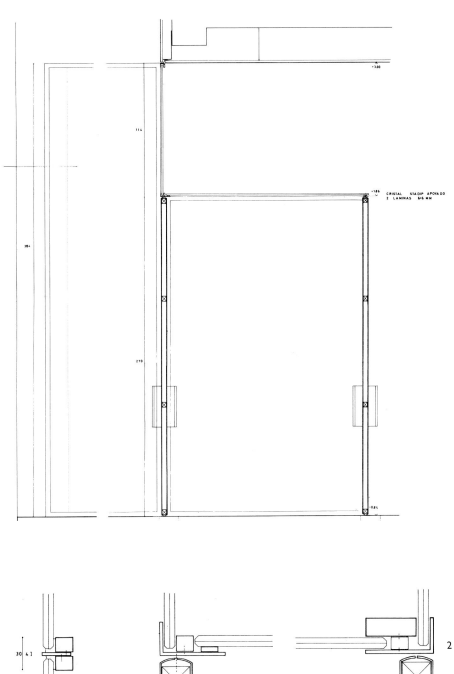

CRISTAL STADIP APOYADO
2 LAMINAS 6+6 MM

2

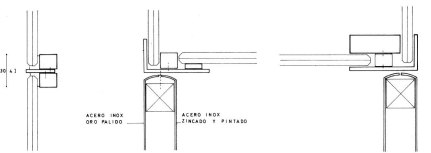

ACERO INOX
ORO PALIDO

ACERO INOX
ZINCADO Y PINTADO

DEVELOPER Spanish Ministry of Justice
SURVEYOR Eduardo González Velayos
INSTALLATIONS ARGU, s.a.
STRUCTURES Juan de la Torre
CONSTRUCTION COMPANY Cubiertas y MZOV

Villanueva de la Cañada Cultural Center

Villanueva de la Cañada. Madrid. Spain
1992-1997

The brief for the Cultural Center commissioned by the Department of Agriculture and Cooperation of the Autonomous Community of Madrid stipulated a program which essentially consisted of four workshops, two classrooms, two gymnasiums, an auditorium for 300 people, a library, and a cafeteria.

These basic functions are distributed in a compact T-shaped building which has been extended outwards through three patios serving, respectively, as a reception area, an exterior extension of the workshops, and an open-air gymnasium. This design focused around courtyards follows the traditional typology used in colonial architecture, which can be found, for instance, around the church and town hall in the center of Villanueva de la Cañada. The open-air spaces considerably enrich the use of the Center, and also announce the public use of the park that extends east of the building, thus generating a previously non-existent activity.

The building is a focus of attraction for the town's citizens, and its architecture is one of the factors producing this attraction. Its organization is sufficiently flexible to house the complex program of a cultural center and its possible changes of use over time.

The space of the large nave is like a canvas-covered plaza with light filtering in from above. In fact, it recalls the typical plazas with temporary lightweight roofing of southern tradition. The image of a universal space protected by this roof creates the feeling of an open, continuous, public place in which the sensation of a unitary experience prevails despite the fact that its use requires its subdivision. The workshops, exhibition area, and adjacent gymnasiums are structurally composed as porticos, organized in modules of 15 meters. These spaces are equipped with natural skylights. The finely finished shop-built roof beams, which are V-shaped and painted white to canalize the light, create environments which are very attractive in their spatial and luminous effects. These elements form a 75 meter-long roof – a structure made up of five groups of six metal V beams, each spanning 15 meters, with an upper flange of concrete. From a constructive viewpoint, the installation of the beams was interesting, given their large dimensions 15 meters long and 2.5 meters high – and their resemblance to boat keels. They were transported separately in special vehicles and mounted individually. Once they were in place, the upper compression flange was fixed in poured concrete.

The exhibition area is also spanned by V-shaped porticos, which are prolonged by a supplement or wing that guarantees an exclusively northern orientation.

1 Area map
2 Sketch
3 Staircase to the library

1

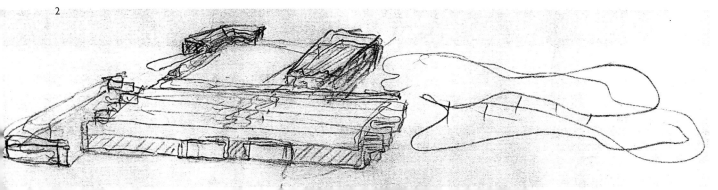

2

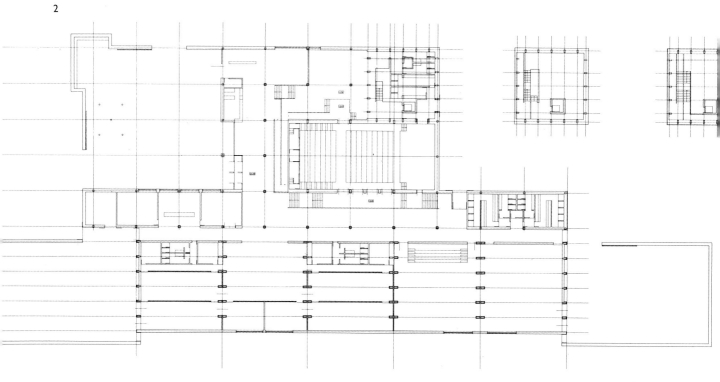

The lateral extremes of the nave's V-shaped beams are enclosed by glazed borders, used here as elements of separation between functions, with large-dimensioned frames of minimal wood sections. The glass offers an uninterrupted view, in which the functional subdivisions of the Cultural Centre – gymnasiums, classrooms, and exhibition hall – do not hinder the visual continuity of the entire upper structure.

Inside the principal nave there are a series of special small classrooms or cabins. Their barrel vault roof of stainless steel reflects the light that filters in through the skylight and diffuses it over the side of the semi-buried auditorium, contributing to the luminous and refined atmosphere of the interior.

The rest of the Center is composed of standard modules measuring 7.5 x 6 meters. The structure of the auditorium, in which the standard module is doubled, consists of beams measuring 12 x 7.5 meters.

The program of the Cultural Center is arranged on a single floor, with the exception of the library, which is developed on two floors. The reading room on the upper floor rises above the rest of the building, thus acting as a belvedere that looks out towards

1 North elevation
2 Floor plans
3 West elevation
4 East elevation
5 Partial view of the north façade

0 I m   I 0m

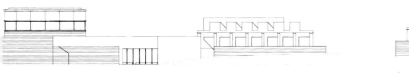

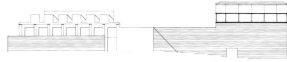

3   4

the park to the east. Its structure is composed of perimeter columns on a 12 x 12 meter base, supporting a roof with beams forming a coffers or a grid.

The finishes distinguish two different zones. The volume of the auditorium and library, as well as the exterior face of the patios, are made of brick. The classrooms, workshops, and the interior face of the patios are finished in white stucco. The brick is laid entirely in headers, with a "Madrid" bond. The 6 mm mortar joints, which are smaller than the norm, required a very exacting control and supervision, in which executed work was inspected daily. In some places, as in the lintels, the brick contains reinforcing bars 4 mm thick, which had to be inserted in the 6 mm joints. No lintel beams or other structural elements interrupt the brick fabric.

The skin can be regarded as a system of curtains which open on penetrating the building. The brick perimeter hides the white stucco forms of the internal volumes and the patio interiors. This principle of concentric rings is not followed in the case of the auditorium, in which the brick appears again as a finish, despite its interior nature, suggesting a new exterior perimeter or patio.

5

1 Workshop corridor
2 Cross section through the auditorium
3 Cross section through the exhibition hall
4 Cross section through the workshops
5 Details of the library section

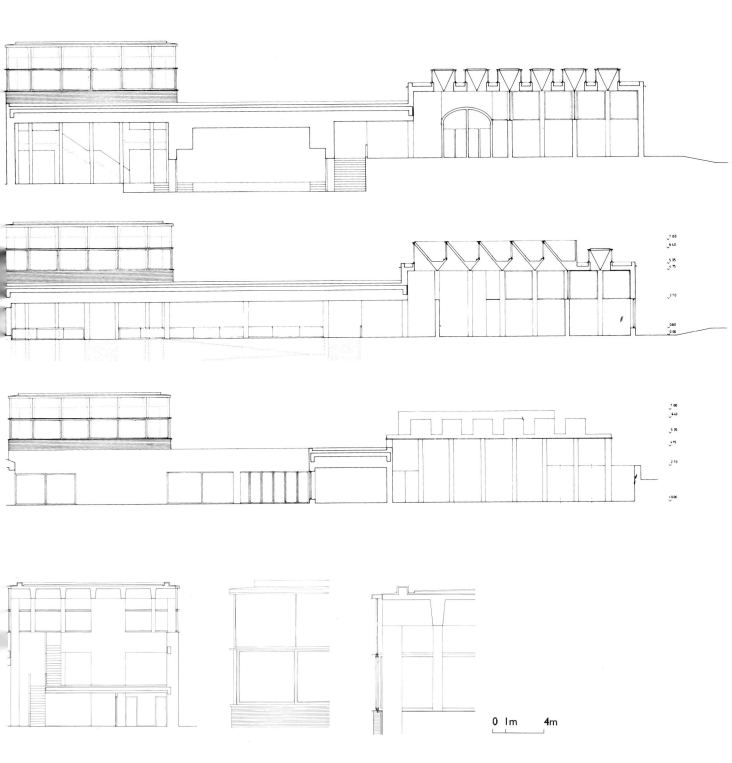

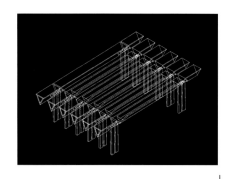

1

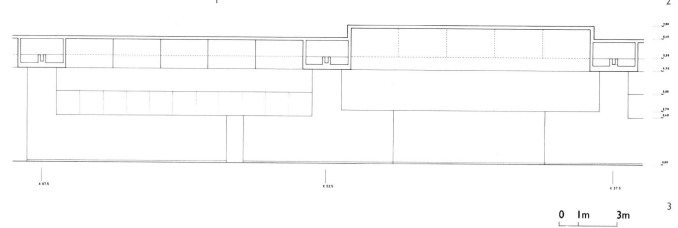

2

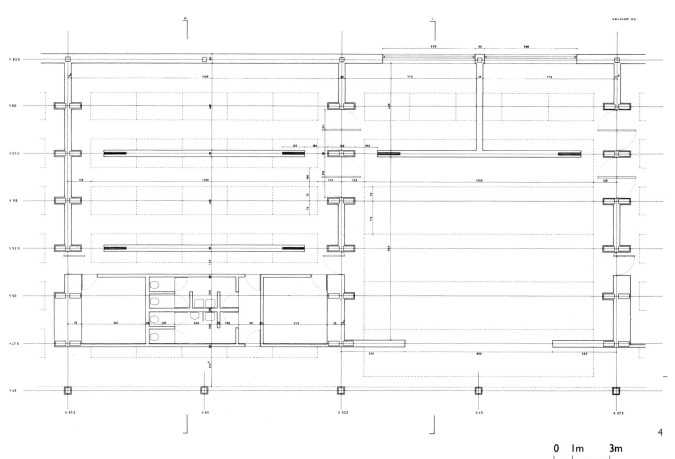

3

4

0   1m   3m

0   1m   3m

5

1 Axonometric drawing of the structure of the exhibition hall

2 Exhibition hall

3 Longitudinal section of the exhibition hall and classroom area

4 Floor plan of the exhibition hall and classroom area

5 Detail of the interior windows separating the exhibiton hall from the classrooms

6 Cross section through the classrooms

7 Cross section through the exhibition hall

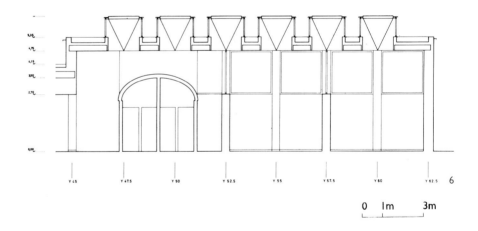

6

0   1m   3m

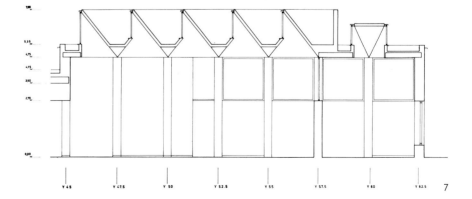

7

DEVELOPER Villanueva de la Cañada Town Hall. Autonomous Community of Madrid
STRUCTURAL CALCULATIONS H.C.A, Juan Francisco de la Torre
CONSTRUCTION COMPANY E.M.E.S.A. Estructuras Mixtas y Edificaciones, S.A.

Woolworth Center of Music Addition

Princeton University
New Jersey. USA
1994-1997

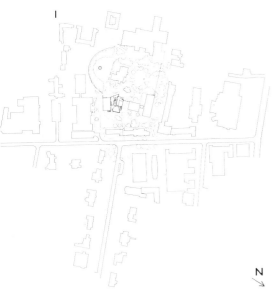

1 Area map

2 Preliminary sketches

3 View from the archway of 1879 Hall

In order to understand the preliminary design presented for the addition and renovation of the Woolworth Center, it is necessary to situate the project within the physical framework of the campus – within the formal structure of Princeton University – in which it is possible to distinguish a superimposition of characteristic patterns.

On a first level, there is a building pattern that extends linearly across the campus, enclosing open spaces. This layout gives rise to a second formal level consisting of a fabric of voids or spaces framed by buildings. Many of these open areas are defined by well-structured and richly tectonic façades articulated in a "college gothic" style. A third level is made up of campus streets and walkways, whose layout sometimes runs parallel to the buildings, while at other times it cuts diagonally across the spaces between them. The geometry of this network of pathways thus reinforces the grid pattern in some cases, while in others it generates a fan-like pattern. The routes that run through the buildings under the archways that are a typical feature of Princeton University form yet another aspect of the pedestrian network. All of these formal levels were present at the site allotted to the Woolworth Center of Music Addition.

The proposal design responds to this context. The new addition houses the library, the new rehearsal room, additional faculty offices and the new administrative suite of the Music Department. The new entrance to the building is situated on the same axis as the existing one. The atrium lobby both embodies the contextual characteristics of the street, covered walkway, route, and plaza, and connects 1879 green and Prospect House yard. At the same time, it acts as a fan that opens out to welcome visitors to the building.

The exterior of the new wing reflects this impulse, originated in the interior space and formalized in the exterior perimeter as a fan-like shape. The northeast corner of the addition gains importance, being as it is the unique image encountered when emerging from the half light of the archway in 1879 Hall.

However, the design for the addition was also conceived as an autonomous entity. Thus, the new Woolworth Center was derived from an internal logic, producing an expansion of the fan that starts to unfold at the transversal lobby axis. In the interior, the building was divided into two halves, with the current teaching wing on one side of the lobby atrium and the new rehearsal hall and library on the other.

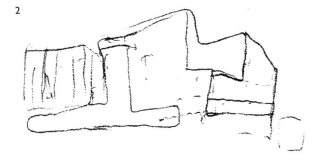

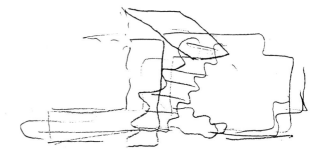

1 East elevation
2 First floor plan
3 View from Prospect Garden
4 View of the lobby atrium from the Prospect
 Garden entry

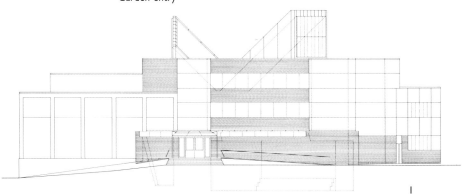

1

2

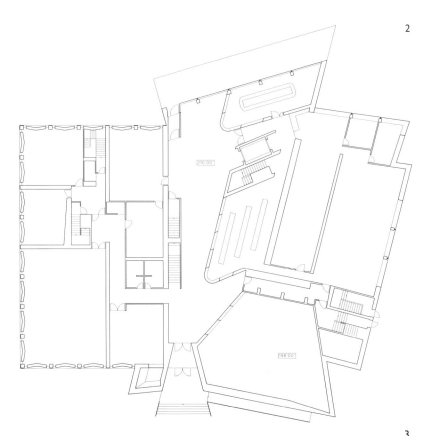

0 1m   5m

3

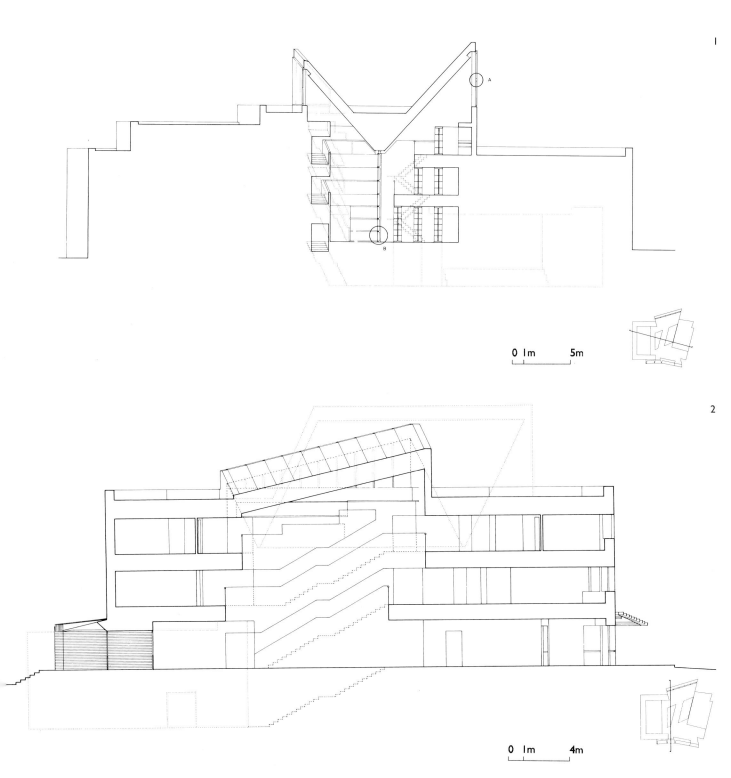

1 Cross section
2 Longitudinal section
3 Sketch
4 View of the lobby atrium from above
Pages 94-95, Rehearsal room

1

A

B

0 1m   5m

2

0 1m   4m

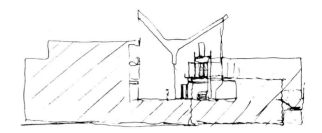

3

4

1 Detail of the curtain wall in the lobby atrium
2 View of the lobby atrium from the 1879
  Green entry

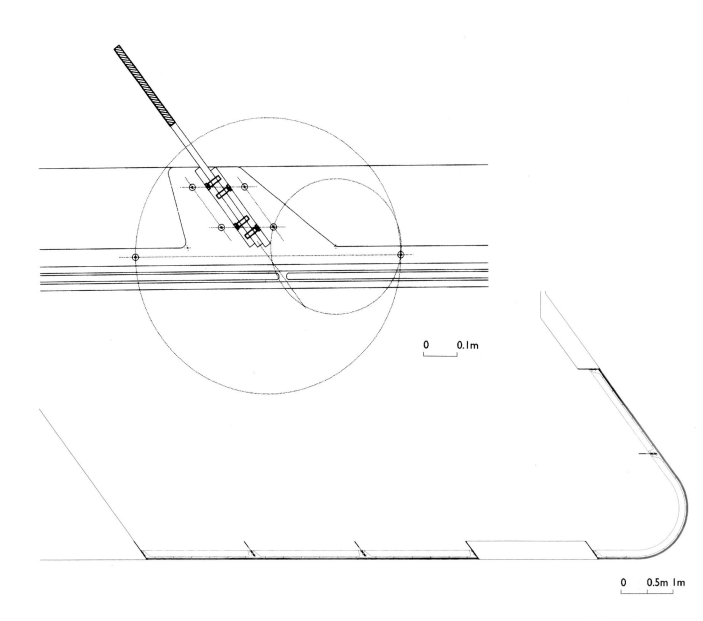

0   0.1m

0   0.5m 1m

COLLABORATING ARCHITECT WASA Architects &
Engineers
PROJECT SUPERVISION WASA, Juan Navarro
Baldeweg, and Enrique Pujana Bambó
STRUCTURAL ENGINEERS Severud Associates,
New York
ACCOUSTICAL CONSULTANTS Achentech, Cambridge,
Massachusetts
LIBRARY CONSULTANT Michael Keller
GENERAL CONTRACTOS Barr & Barr, New York

Competition for the Island of Museums

Berlin. Germany
1994

The need to create a unified organizational scheme for the museum complex on the island requires a global reconsideration of the historic site, located in the heart of Berlin. The problem presented by this densely structured ensemble calls for a solution that does not entail the use of architecture as an additional object. It seems unnecessary to add new buildings to the crowded massing of the complex. Instead, the problem should be treated with complementary criteria designed to establish a system – a multi-dimensional network – of connections between the buildings. One of the first and most important ideas of the proposal focuses on the treatment of the ground plane as one of these dimensions – as an architectonic material. The competition design thus recreates a landscape that endows the existing buildings with a new source of support: a ground plane, covered with grass, on a double slope which forms a gentle hill designed to distinguish the site. From this elevation, the buildings appear to be slightly sunken, thereby losing weight and volume, and the connection between earth and architecture is increased. The appearance of the ensemble of buildings thus gains in flexibility and malleability. Rising in the low relief of the artificial ground plane, the forms seem to emerge from the interior of the island.

The sum of the interventions executed on the island over time has endowed the site with an additive character. It is now necessary to compensate for this character with subtractive interventions: to create depressed areas in the hill, to excavate patios or fissures, in short, to implement actions that "carve" and "cut away" balancing the "modeling" of the complex. The result of this process will create a more harmonious ensemble in which the museums will be intimately linked to the place.

1 Area map
2 Model of the proposal

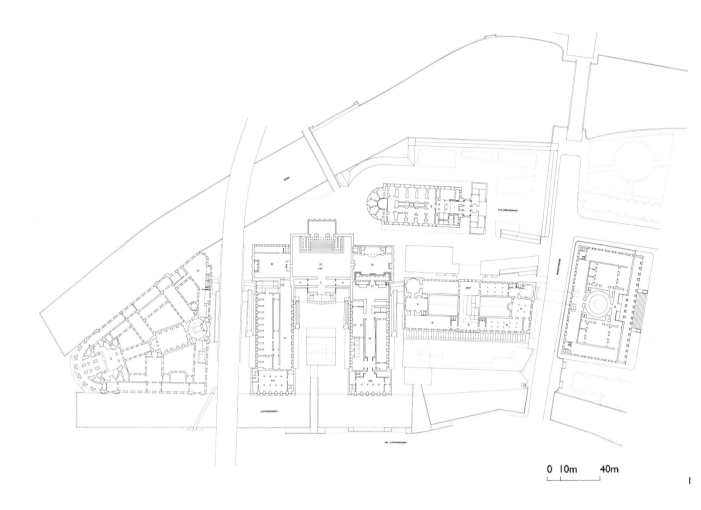

0 10m   40m

1

1 General floor plan
2 Roof plan
3 Model of the proposal

The artificial hill also connects the spaces and vestibules of the museums – the Neues Museum, the Pergamon Museum and the Bode Museum – without tunnels or passages, thereby achieving a continuous organizing structure.

The proposal introduces a geometry that brings together the different interventions and the gardens. This geometry follows the guidelines of a regulating grid, which has its origins in the form and position of Schinkel's Altes Museum, and which is intended to integrate the buildings of the island in a single generative impulse.

The Museum Island is connected to the city via a system of bridges over the canal, from Am Kupfergraben Street on the eastern side to the small park. The island is also accessible by boat. In the design, the existing network of docks is increased with a new pier in front of the Pergamon Museum. The grand marquees in front of the Neues and Pergamon Museums, arranged linearly, shelter the principal entrance and reception areas. These house the control areas, information desks, stores, coatrooms and cafeterias. The use of a network of skylights makes it possible for natural light to filter into the large lobby area created under the museums. The skylight system is laid out following the guidelines of the regulating grid. The axis of the vestibules is defined by the shafts of light that open around the walls of the Pergamon Museum. The exhibition halls are easily accessed from the reception areas. From the entrance to the Pergamon Museum, an attractive skylit passage leads to the large space housing the Pergamon Altar in what is called the "short" circuit. The rooms exhibiting the Temple of King Sahure and of Nefertiti, located in the Neues Museum, are connected to the area that leads up to the hall of Babylon. This entry allows visitors to follow the correct processional route.

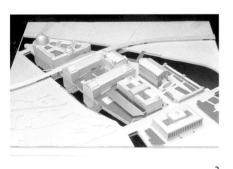

3

In our view, the rehabilitation of the Neues Museum should follow strict reconstruction criteria to attain the greatest architectural fidelity possible, except for irrecoverable details and ornaments. A modern reinterpretation is thus avoided, reconfiguring the façades to their original form and rejecting a bridge connection to the Altes Museum. Schinkel's museum is a building of extraordinary beauty, whose exquisite proportions should glow in their autonomous singularity. This seems to us imperative, despite the initial project designed by Stüler. In our proposal, the connection between the Neues and the Altes Museum is made under the Bodestrasse. The former hall places the aedicule of the caryatids on the transverse axis, emphasizing the route connecting the museums and enabling the Neues Museum to maintain an inherent flexibility and a composition of symmetrical effects congruent with its autonomous nature.

The gardens surrounding the National Museum are organized according to the geometric guidelines of the complex, creating links that ensure their formal relation to the Altes Museum, on one side, and the Neues Museum, on the other. The proposal is also comfortably integrated into the city fabric. The existing skyline formed by the buildings is preserved and views from a distance remain uninterrupted by intervening constructions. To the contrary, the gentle slopes of grass and the marquees favor these visual escapes, providing a sense of natural-ness and completeness to the whole. Finally, the transformed landscape of the island is chromatically enriched. The grey and neutral tonality of the buildings is underscored by the green grass of the hill, the silvery enclosure of the marquees, the red brick paving of the bridges, and the lively reflections of the skylights, which punctuate the entire space.

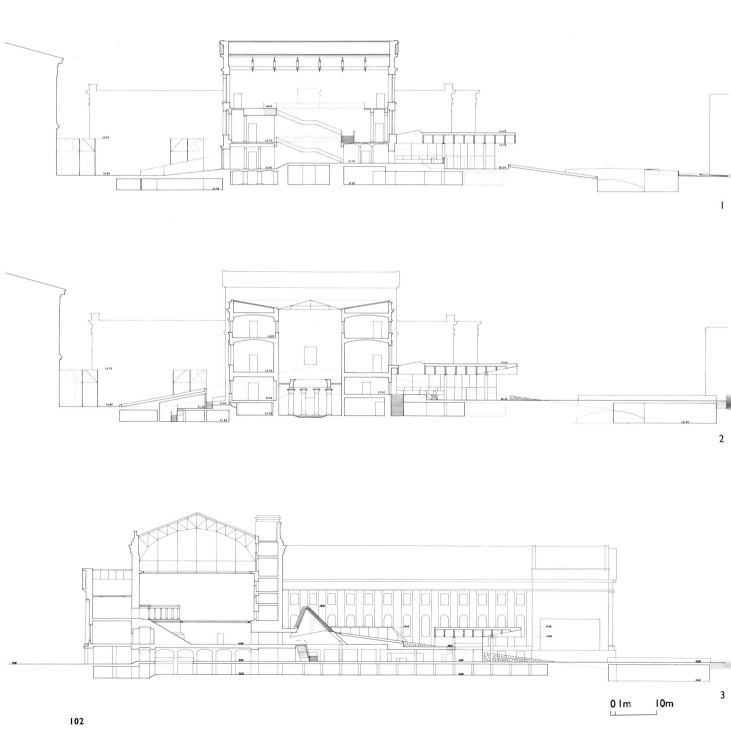

1

2

3

0 1m   10m

4

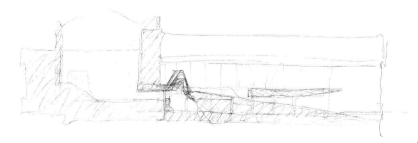

5

Salvador Allende Museum and Cultural Center

Santiago de Chile. Chile
1993

The plot assigned to the new Cultural Center occupies a steeply inclined terrain that stands out symbolically in the urban fabric. The site, integrated into the Metropolitano Park, enjoys panoramic vistas and dominates the surrounding landscape. The design solves the program through the creation of a complex physical ensemble of heterogeneous elements whose diversity is strongly related to the concrete position they occupy in the topography and the functions they accommodate. The museum dominates the complex in particularly transcendent fashion, appearing as a freestanding element on the large terrace created at its base – an ample open-air room from which the museum overlooks the city.

The auditorium located below the terrace can be accessed through either the museum or through an independent entrance from the street for car traffic. The auditorium area corresponds to an excavation bordered by light, undulating metal surfaces which are distanced from the image of containing walls by the fact that they do not reach all the way down to the ground. A pedestrian route opens between the two ensuing curvilinear forms.

The Center offers a lively image to the city, inviting exploration and incursion. A large, lightly stepped sheet of water increases the material richness of this urban frontier.

The design for the museum results from its structure and from a consideration of the appropriate entry of natural sky light. The space consists of a succession of porticos of large dimensions, made of post-tensioned concrete, which leave the exhibition area free of columns. The perimeter that defines the area under the roof moves freely

in relation to this over-embracing square-plan structure, creating a series of open spaces or, simply, mediation places between the museum and the ample platform of halls.

Inside, the building accommodates a temporary exhibition hall and a permanent collection area. A passage of light – a narrow sunlit border – cuts across the unitary space of the museum. This effect is created through a change in the orientation of the screens which are incorporated in the large beams to filter and direct natural light. This path of light alone, without any other physical definitions, marks out the main route through the museum and, at the same time, separates the exhibition areas. The solution warrants complete freedom in the use and occupation of the space. Complementary service areas such as workshops, libraries and administration offices are mainly housed in a parallel rectangular wing, which accompanies and announces the containing walls of the ramps and stairs for circulation on the upper part of the site. These circulation routes, ramps and stairs are organized into itineraries which offer contrasting and variable spatial experiences. The project is rich in its exterior spaces, alternating experiences of confinement with others of uncluttered space open to ample horizons. The view of the complex from above, from the summit of Mount San Cristóbal, was also carefully considered in the design of the roof and artificial relief. The Salvador Allende Cultural Center – which is adapted to the site and, at the same time, is autonomous in its main elements – will offer a variable image to this landscape. It will be an integrated and attractive physical ensemble.

1 Area map
2 Sketch of the ensemble

N

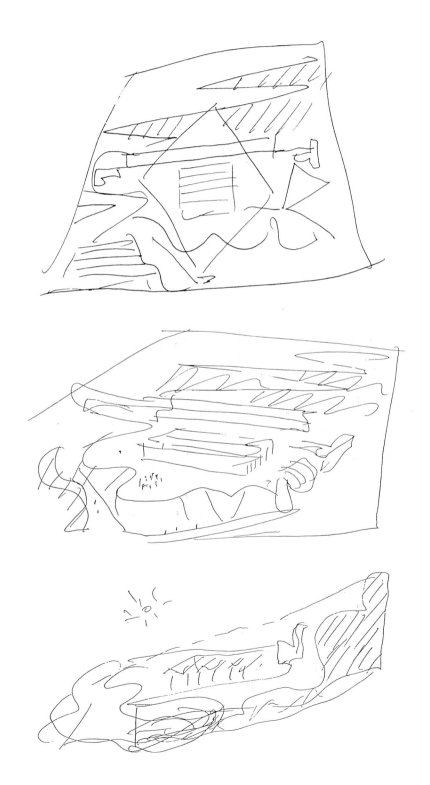

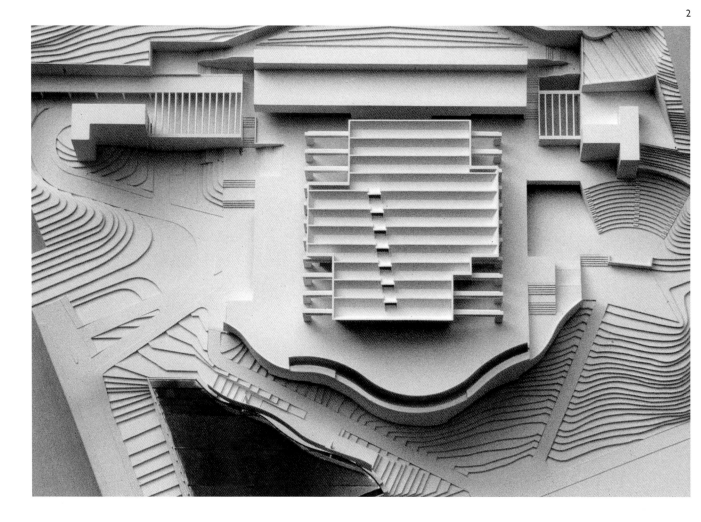

1 Sketch
2 Model
3 General floor plan

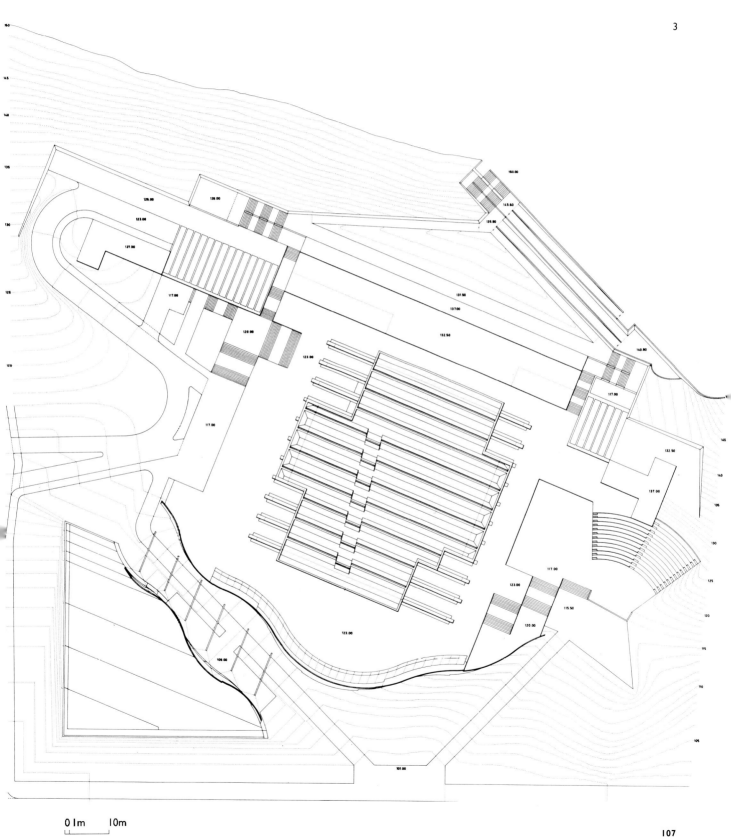

0 1m   10m

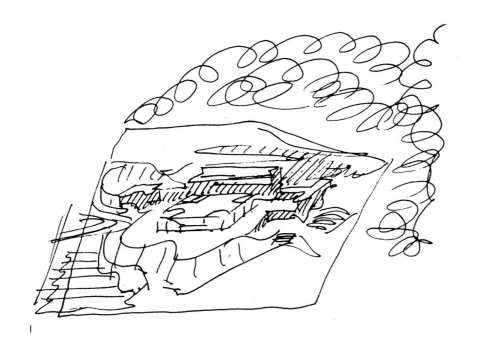

1

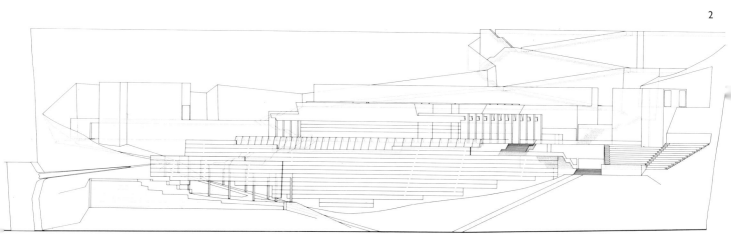

2

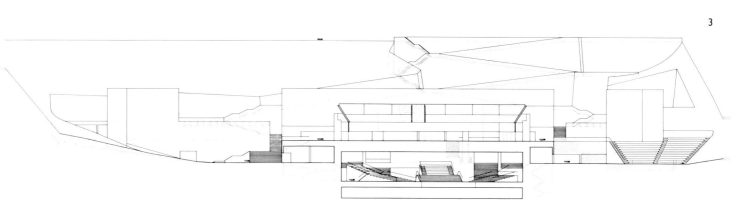

3

0 1m   10m

4

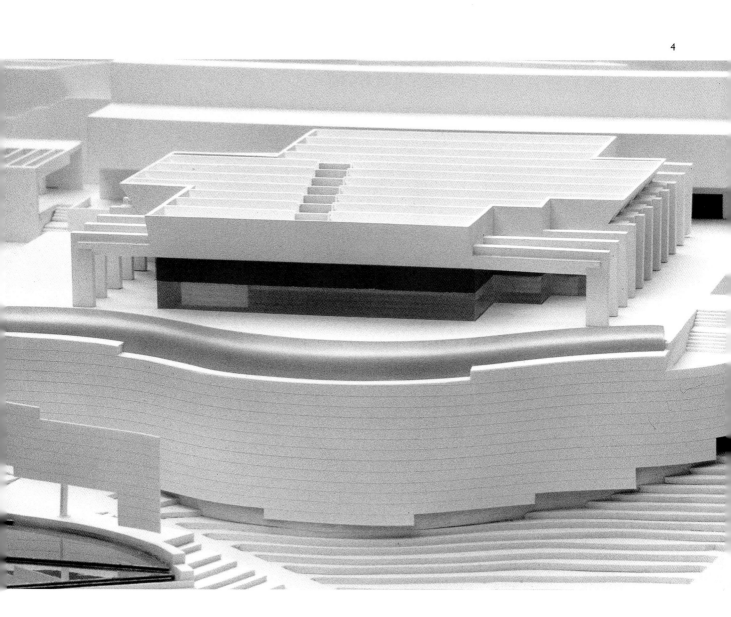

1

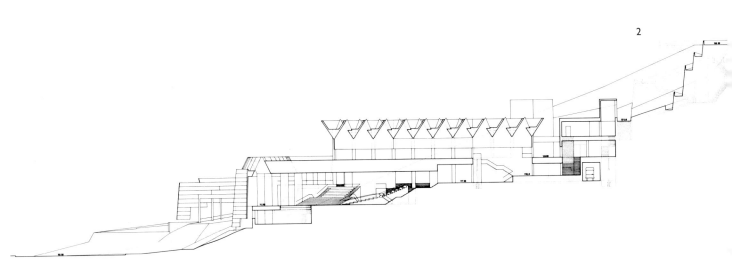

2

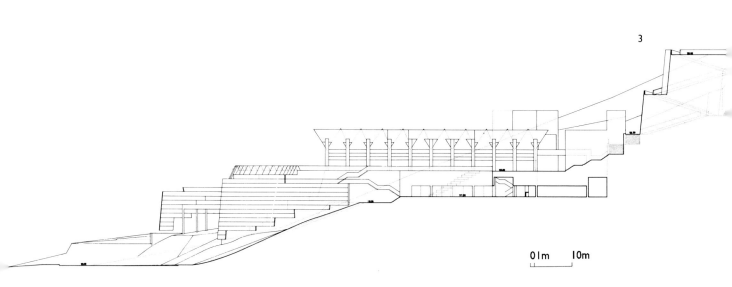

3

01m   10m

1 Sketch

2 Cross section through the museum and the
  auditorium

3 Cross section through the path leading up to
  Mount San Cristóbal

4 Detail of the model

4

Preliminary Ideas for the Arrecife Marina Project

Lanzarote. Canary Islands. Spain
1998

1 Area map
2 Model of the proposal

My architect's vision for the city of Arrecife is a personal interpretation that responds to several impulses. In the first place it reflects evident social needs which demand physical interventions designed to create cultural infrastructures and housing. But it also answers to an idea of the city – to an integral, desired model in which nature and the unique characteristics of the territory play a primordial role.

This proposal has therefore been motivated by the desire to both meet a program of needs and offer a more satisfactory and pleasant life-style for the citizens of Arrecife, taking into account the area's marvelous natural environment, which should be treated with the greatest respect.

Arrecife's coastal form weaves a very complex web of water and earth – concave and convex areas of sea or shore. The coast, which is low-lying, advances and retreats, transforming what encircles into what is encompassed, positive into negative, figures of water into shapes of earth. We contemplate this dual tension of terrestrial accidents and marine areas. This physical metamorphosis, that makes islands of earth and pools of water apparently interchangeable, is characteristic of Arrecife. Thus the Pool of San Ginés appears in duality with the Island of El Francés, as do the

↑N

islets of Fermina and Castillo, or the bays of Arrecife and Juan Rejón. And the salt flats, once recovered and filled with water, will offer an image of an archipelago – of islands of water scattered across dry land.

The proposal focuses mainly on the area of the Pool of San Ginés, the Island of El Francés, the Port of Naos, and a large area currently occupied by warehouses that extends to the abandoned salt flats to the north. Intervention in this extensive area of Arrecife is considered to be both decisive and necessary, since it offers the greatest potential advantage to be gained from its urbanization and evident possibilities for urban life.

1

1 Model of the interior of the Maritime
  Museum
2 Sketches
3 Section through the auditorium and museum
  at the Pool of San Ginés

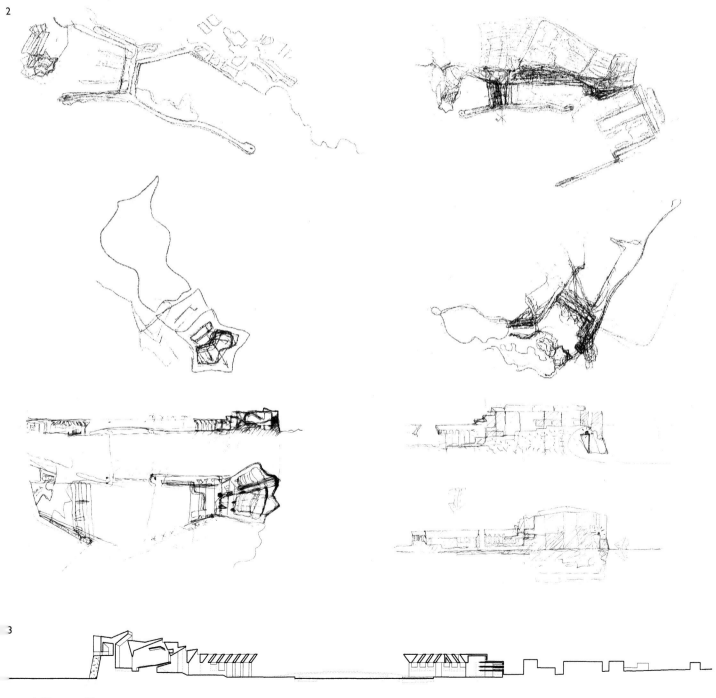

2

3

0 10m   50m

1

2

0 10m   50m

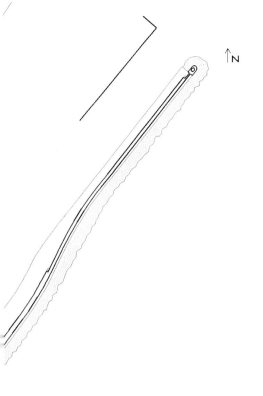

1 General distribution plan for the Island of El
  Francés and the Port of Naos
2 Longitudinal section
3 Model of the Maritime Museum

PROPOSAL DEVELOPER César Manrique
Foundation

3

Urban Rehabilitation Project for Turin

Nine Projects for Nine Cities

Milan Triennial, Italy

1986

The shape and scale of the River Dora as it passes through Turin are used to generate the layout and dimensions of the proposed new buildings, as well as the general configuration of the park and open spaces between them. The natural topography and the form cut by the river are given protagonism in the design, reproducing the descent to the river as a grand urban gesture. Two geometries dominate this part of the city: the curvilinear course of the river, and the urban grids that intersect it with difficulty. The solution adopted seeks to create a balance between the two geometries and the new buildings, as well as to frame the structures that are conserved in a play of tensions between their autonomous identity

and their continuity in the natural forms and the urban fabric. One of the points of difficulty in the union of the river bed and the street grid can be appreciated in their tangential contact along Corso Umbria. In response to this uncomfortable tangency, we have followed a strategy of amplification, creating a large pool parallel to the street. The tangency is thus transformed artificially into a parallelism between the course of the water and the street, and the conflict between the urban grid and the river is solved by making their contact more evident and deliberate along their entire length. An old mill, together with the installations for the irrigation channel that it served, mark one end of the great pool, dedicated

1 Area map of the ensemble

2 Illustration of the proposal

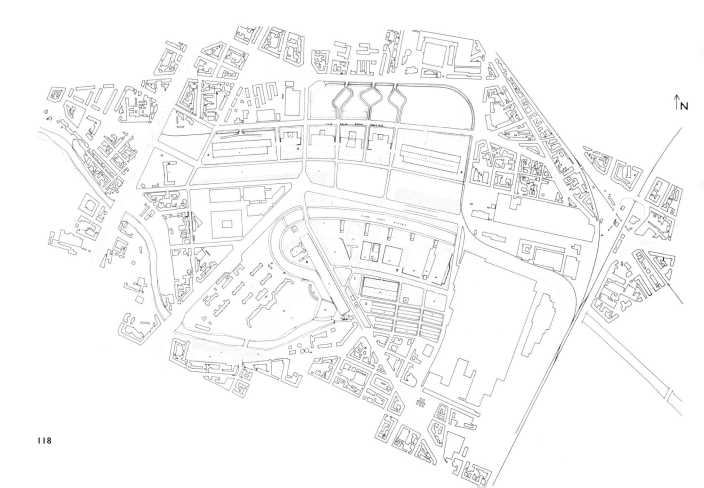

1 Detail of the model
2 Fragment of the plan for the new industrial,
  business, and auditorium zone

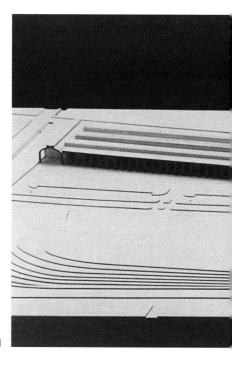

1

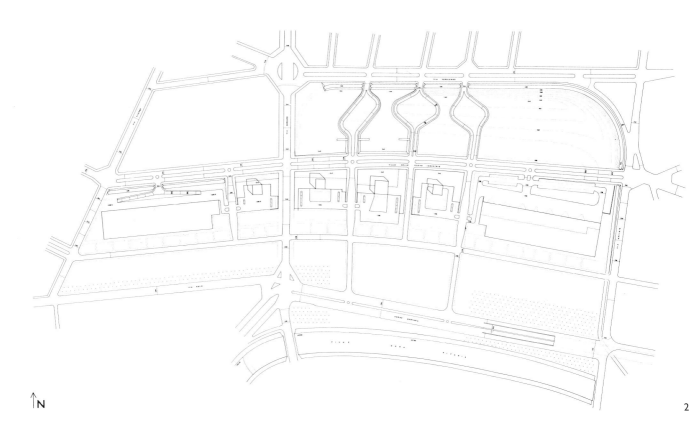

N

2

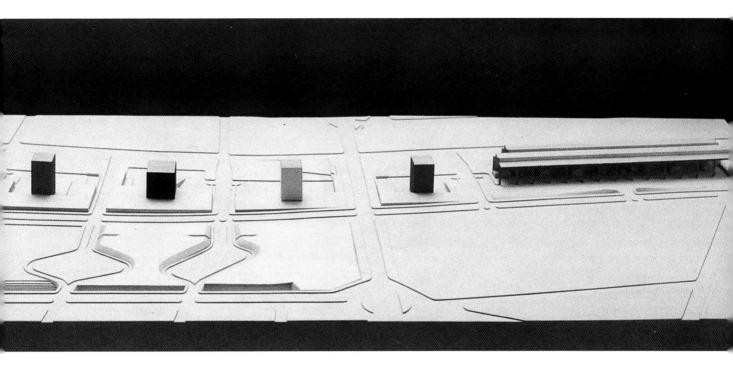

to recreational uses. This complex acts as an instrument of harmonization. Its concrete exposition is an example of the general attitude adopted towards the rehabilitation of the urban fabric. Fundamentally, the project can be seen as a large green area in which the program activities are developed as open and punctual events. The program is solved with recreational facilities; new industrial installations which involve, in part, the rehabilitation of industrial warehouses; a residential area on Via Trevisa that continues the urban fabric in the southern zone; and a commercial area. In each industrial zone, existing elements are conserved, and certain fragments remodeled. In this way, the memory of a specific use and physical reminders of a handsome rational architecture are maintained. The modular and repetitive nature of this architecture permits its fragmentary rehabilitation without loss of value.

The program is completed by a series of small towers designed to accommodate offices, laboratories, and meeting rooms to support the new activities in the rehabilitated workshops or warehouses.

Our objective has been to maintain a complex balance between contradictory demands. The scope of the program, which is adequate for a city the size of Turin, introduces a new activity that does not exclude family life or general, public life. In the proposal, we avoid the physical rupture which would have created a void, on the one hand, or a completely closed construction, indifferent to the need for open space suggested by the river, on the other. The design has therefore been guided by the desire to give a sense of naturalness to the encounter between the free and natural texture of the river valley and the fabric of the city that has grown in its midst.

1 Elevation of the sports zone

2 Cross section through the sports zone

3 Floor plan of the tiered seating and changing room level of the sports center and pool

4 Models of the sports center and the covered swimming pool

5 Detail of the sports, commercial, and residential zone model

1

2

0 1m   5m

3
4

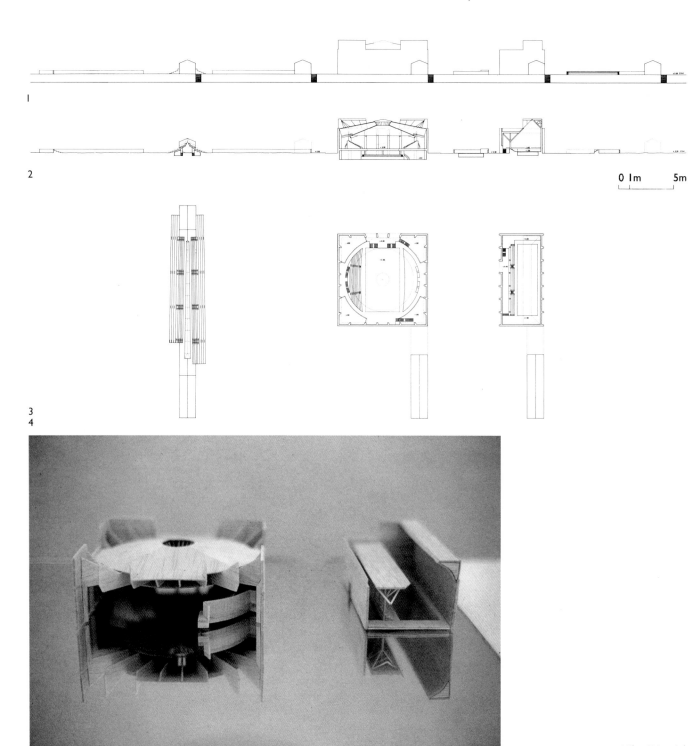

DEVELOPER Milan Triennial

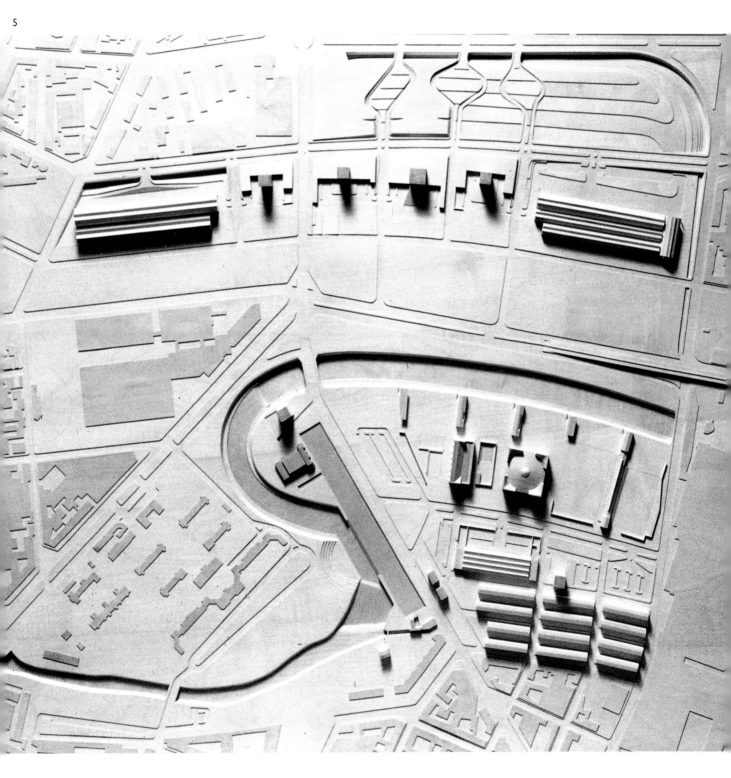

Urban Rehabilitation Project for the Nordbahnhofgelände

Vienna. Austria
1991

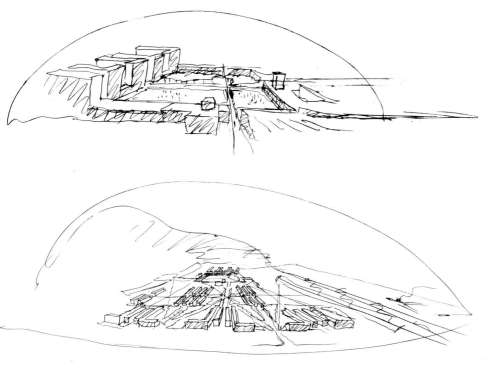

1 Preliminary sketches

2 Area map

This urban rehabilitation project proposes a complex and mixed structure of simple and differentiated elements. Residential buildings, office spaces, car and pedestrian networks, parks, and gardens are physically superimposed in a structure whose layered nature makes it possible to establish a topological distinction between the areas generated by each separate social activity. In this way, the design manages to create a social space that is flexible, variable, and subtle in its contact with the public and the private spheres.

The entire area opens from Lassalle Street, in a system made up of parks and developed blocks, forming a chessboard grid that is diagonally crossed by pedestrian walkways.

In the design, the modeling of the ground plays a decisive role worthy of special mention. The alternation in the elevation of the ground – the change in level of the terrain – has important repercussions on the visual horizon of the users. The entire area has been treated like a low-relief sculpture. Around the residential blocks, park areas have been situated on the upper level, about three meters above the street network designed for car traffic.

This arrangement, which uses very soft forms to lend continuity to the different spaces, can be appreciated in the section. The diagonal walks, developed on this upper level, achieve an uninterrupted visual appropriation of the area, which the pedestrian can continuously enjoy.

The typical urban block is formed by two parallel volumes. One, at the level of the street, houses office spaces. The other, on the upper level overlooking

N

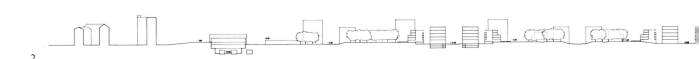

the gardens, accommodates houses and apartments.

A very large and slightly sunken plaza acts as the focal point for a commercial center, which serves both this area and the surrounding neighborhoods. This large plaza is separated from the upper, more private plane of the residential parks, thus avoiding any possible conflict and interference in its use. The sports and recreation area can be found in the park closest to this plaza. By moving the station to one side and burying the tracks, the Praterstern is freed from the train and restructured to accommodate a complex of new buildings, arranged in a fan, for commercial and institutional uses.

The decision to move the train station to one side, albeit costly, is supported by the central character that this plaza can develop in the future, taking into account the bifocal condition of Vienna as it has developed towards the northeast, on the other side of the Danube. The Praterstern thus becomes a center along the axis marked by Prater and Lassalle Streets.

The border defined by the Nordbahnstrasse in this area has been carefully designed to assure the continuity of traffic beyond the buried train lines through the reorientation of the street grid in the western section of the project area.

The river edge has also been largely redesigned to incorporate a linear park dotted with platforms overlooking the river, and a longitudinal canal offering an immediate experience of water in Handels Kay.

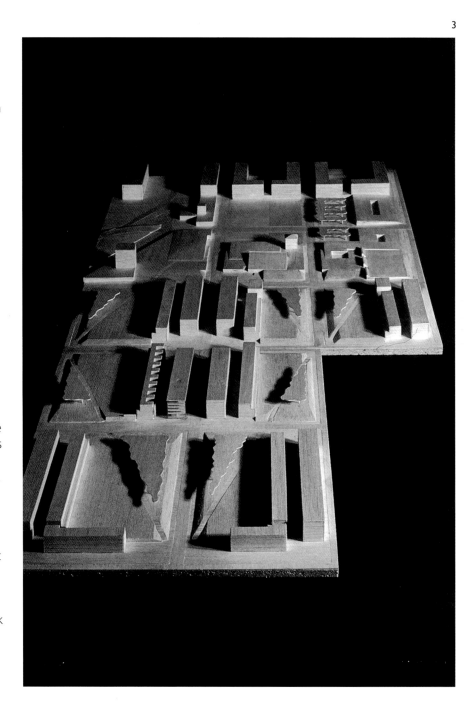

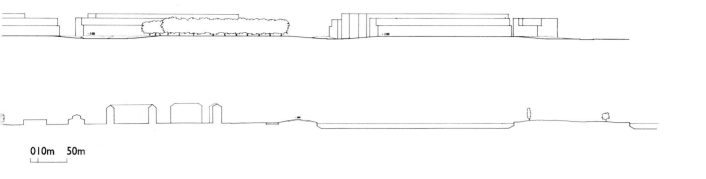

010m 50m

4

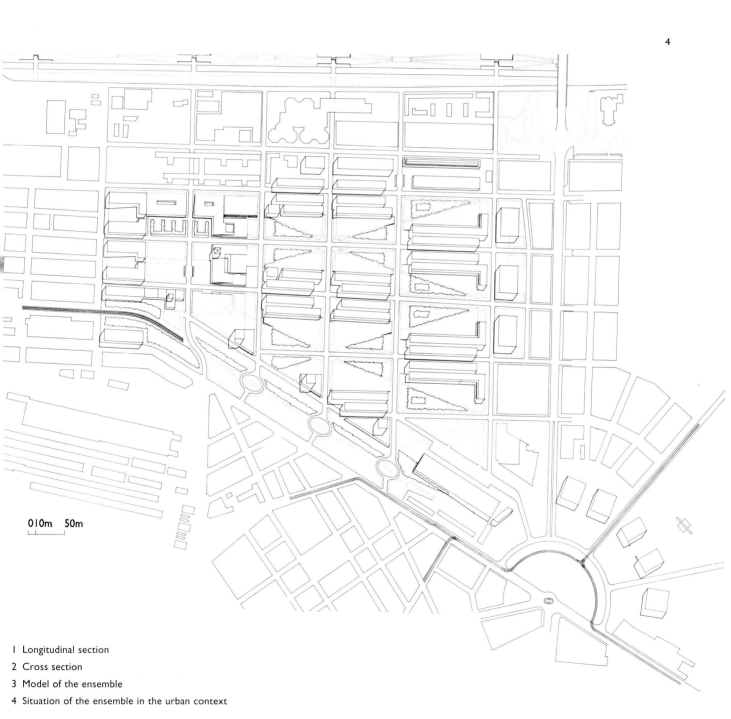

010m 50m

1 Longitudinal section
2 Cross section
3 Model of the ensemble
4 Situation of the ensemble in the urban context

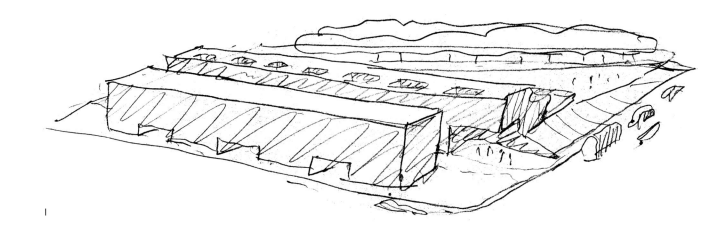

1

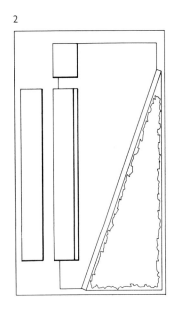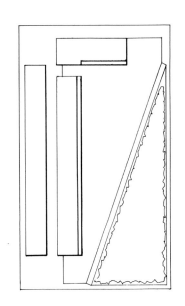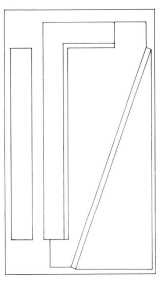

2

0 10m   50m

3

0 10m 20m

1 Sketch of typical urban block

2 Scheme of possible urban block volume
distribution alternatives

4 Cross section through typical urban block

3 Park system

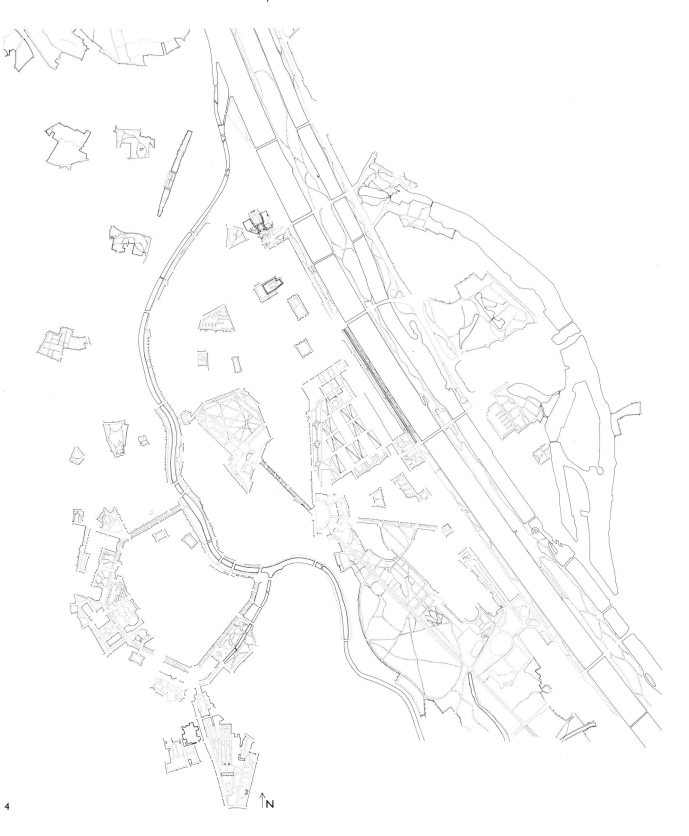

4

↑N

Salzburg Covention Center

Salzburg. Austria
1992

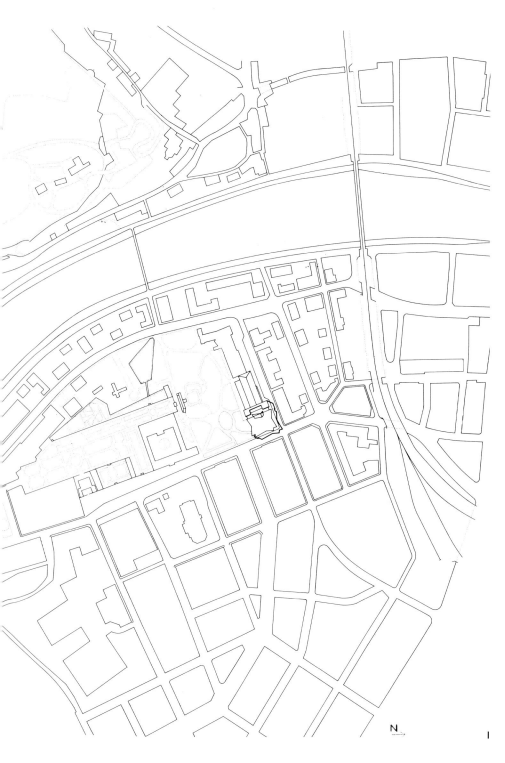

One of the most prominent features of the Salzburg Center is its star-shaped form, which is clad in metallic vestments the color of pale gold.

Designed to stand opposite Mirabell Palace, it appears as a complementary figure of the royal venue, with which it establishes a dialogue while, at the same time, remaining differentiated and independent. Its geometry evokes the broken polygons of the fortifications that once surrounded the old palace in a condensed and reduced form.

The surface in which the Convention Center is wrapped has been designed to actively display itself, shining brilliantly and attracting the gaze as one approaches from Rainerstrasse. The presence of this luminous polyhedron will notably enrich the experience of the place, bringing together distant associations and the sensuality of new materials.

The project accepts the complexity and specificity of the proposed program without losing clarity in its organization, and without undermining its sense of unity. At the same time, it encompasses the different characters of a convention center, on the one hand, and a hotel, on the other.

The site has been opened to the park and Rainerstrasse. The main entrance to the Center is situated along this street, making it permeable to both the park and the street, which enter into the site.

The ground floor of the building accommodates the entrance lobby, the principal accesses, and the cafeteria and restaurant, which overlook the park. The most visible and commercial corner, formed by the intersection of Rainerstrasse and Auerspergstrasse, is given over to commercial spaces.

N

1 Area map
2 Preliminary sketch
3 Model of the proposal as seen from the park

2
3

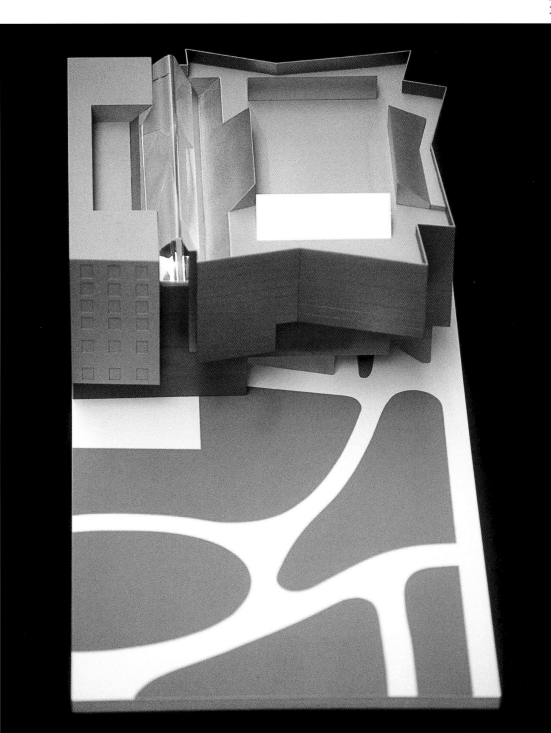

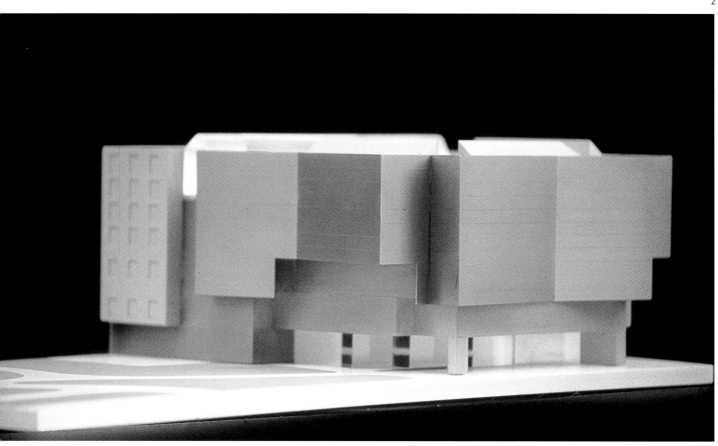

1 Roof plan
2 Model as seen from Rainerstrasse
3 Floor plan, level +15.60
4 Floor plan, level 0.00

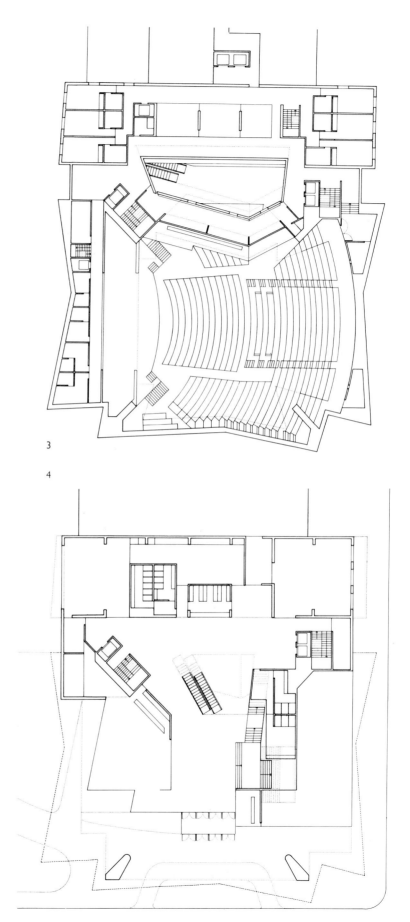

3

4

0 1m   5m

1 Longitudinal section through the hall
2 Cross section through the atrium and hall
3 Model of the Hotel and Convention Center
  as seen from the park

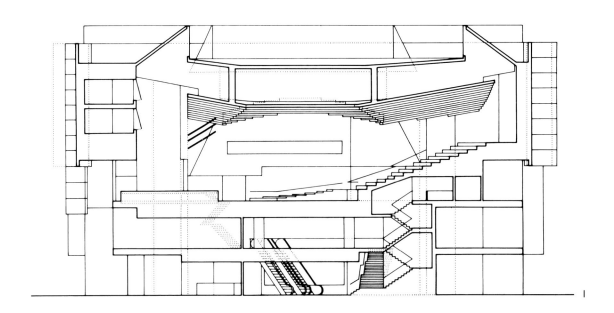

1

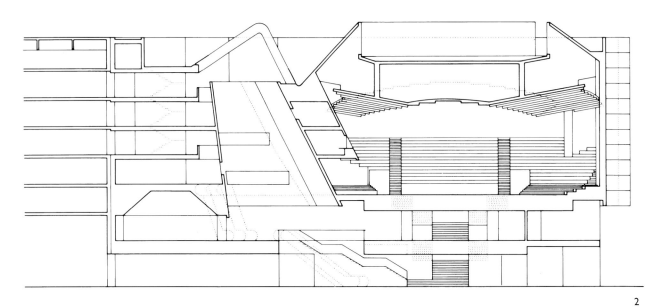

2

0 1m   5m

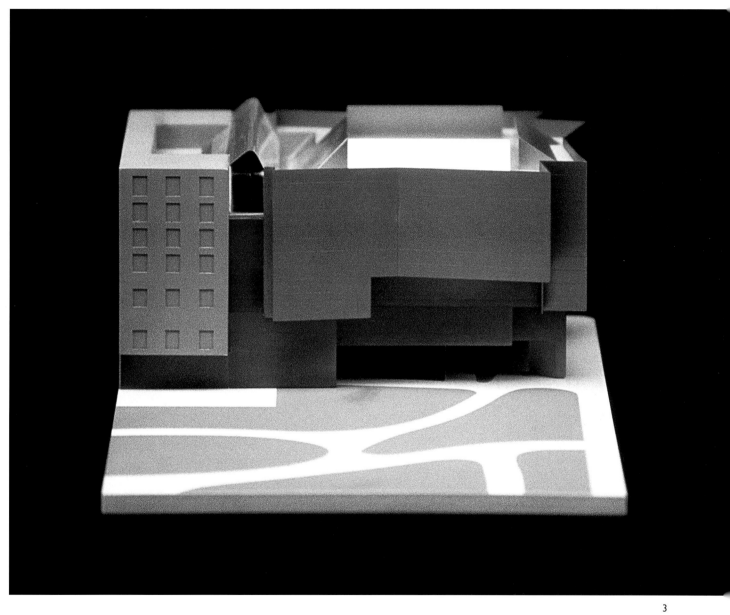

3

Hertziana Library

Rome. Italy
1995

A rehabilitation project for the area that was once the garden of the Zuccari Palace requires, above all, that special attention be given to the physical roots of this singular space laden with history. It would be difficult not to act in consonance with the *genius loci*, which will always try to make itself visible and manifest in any respectful intervention.

The place, which was already a terraced garden in the Roman Villa of Lucullus, is generated by the stepped arrangement of the containing walls that descend along the southern side of the slopes of Pincio. The informal references suggested by this garden, whose staggered layout offers a unified vision of the site, have inspired our project.

In our design, public access to the new library takes place through the Mascherone Gate, a figure that was for Zuccari a necessary contrast to the paradisiacal charm that unfolds and is left open to view upon crossing its threshold.

In our case, too, the general constitution of the library becomes immediately understandable from this entry point. The place appears metamorphosed into a well of light with a glazed perimeter, along whose slightly inclined background wall the light cascades in and reflects out. A series of stepped terraces with a free perimeter outline, designed to contain the bookcases and reading rooms, have been arranged around this central element. Although small, the resulting interior

1

1 Mascherone Gate
2 Area map
3 Model. View from the main lobby

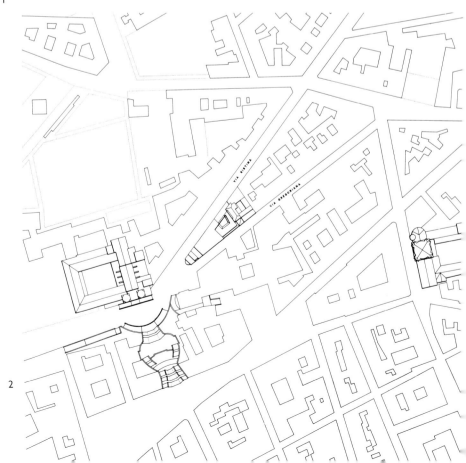

2

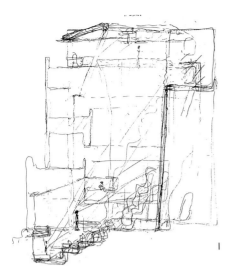

area is spatially interesting in its vertical unfolding, in its luminous ambiance, and in the formal richness of a stepped organization with a trapezoidal profile.

The different floors are organized following a regular distribution, which places the book stacks in the area facing Via Sixtina, and the reading areas in the area looking over Via Gregoriana, beside the windows and terraces that open to a panoramic view of Rome.

A room for silent reading is located on the upper floor as a segregated activity, independent from the high central common space. This room also benefits from an upper terrace, a place to rest and enjoy the views.

The transition from the lowest terrace of Stroganoff Palace to the high terrace of Zuccari Palace is resolved via a conventional sloping roof. This permits an easier connection to be made, and smoothens the broken profile of the entire Hertziana Library complex. This roof is combined with skylight elements, which ensure good natural lighting in the upper silent reading room.

The proposal reveals our intention

to give variety to the roof plan, accepting the fragmentation and the coexistence of flat terraces and inclined planes which is typical of the roofs of Rome, as seen in aerial views of the city.

The proposed finish for the walls that enclose the high central space is exposed whitewashed brick. Its texture invites one to recall the interior of the Glipoteca in Munich.

The light tone of the whitewashed brick should act as an effective reflector of the skylight, tinting the atmosphere with a warm and luminous color. On the entrance floor, the paving will be travertine marble, and on upper levels, the floors will be largely of wood.

The simple and noble character of the finishes – the whitewashed brick, the stone, the wood, and even the presence of the books as a visible skin – should create a system of materials in mutual harmony, enhancing the pleasant atmosphere of the ensemble.

2

0 1m   5m

1 Sketch
2 Floor plan, level 0.00
3 Model. View of the courtyard and lobby
  from the second floor
4 Via Gregoriana elevation

3

4

0 1m   5m

1 Section

2 Detail of the model. View of the entrance
from the upper levels

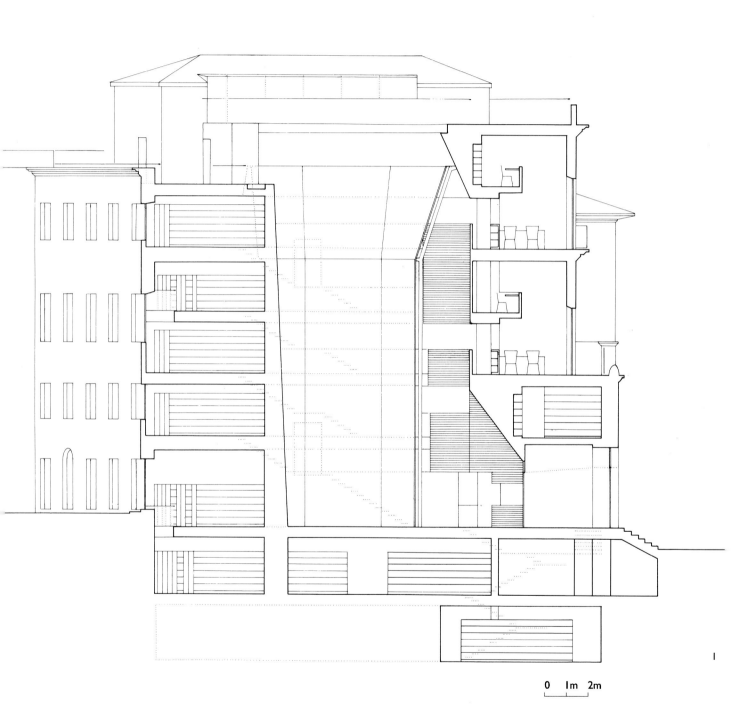

0   1m 2m

1

2

DEVELOPER Max-Planck-Gesellschaft zur
Förderung der Wissenschaften E. V.

Altamira Museum and Research Center

Santillana del Mar. Santander. Spain
1994-2000

Several years ago, conservation problems in the cave of Altamira made it necessary to impose restrictions on the number of visitors to the site. The situation also pointed to the need to build a center designed to house the research facilities and headquarters of the Altamira Trust.

A study of the state of the site, and ensuing evidence of its deterioration, led to the decision to build a replica of the cave, in the environs of the original site, in order to absorb the large influx of visitors which Altamira could no longer accommodate.

The new research center – a unified version of the one which was spread out among several pavilions and was consequently handicapped functionally – had to be located beside the replica. In addition, a museum had to be built in response to the new needs of dissemination and expectations of public visitors to the site. Spaces for a library and storage rooms for the archeological holdings also had to be integrated into the new complex. These exhibition and storage facilities had to have sufficient capacity to hold on deposit the collection of Paleolithic Prehistory of the Regional Museum of Prehistory and Archeology of Cantabria.

It thus became necessary not only to plan the presence of the building in the landscape, but also to consider a series of complementary actions with a view to warranting the conservation of the cave's original environs, including the proper organization of the massive flow of visitors in order to cause minimal damage to the site.

The commission brief stipulated the need to locate the new research center and museum close to the original cave of Altamira, to house a program of considerable size and, at the same time, to make an in-depth study of the formal characteristics of the work in order to respect the fragile landscape. Care had to be taken to maintain the original uncluttered appearance of the landscape surrounding the cave, thereby preserving the evocative and mysterious atmosphere that it required.

1 Preliminary sketch
2 Model of the proposal

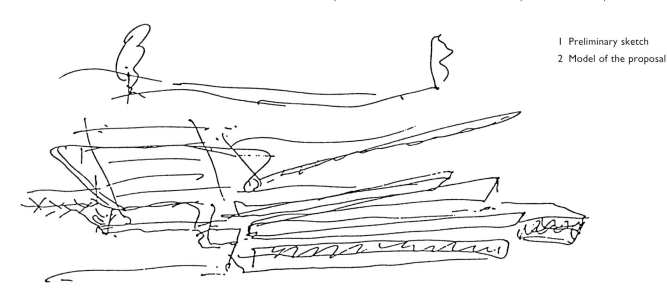

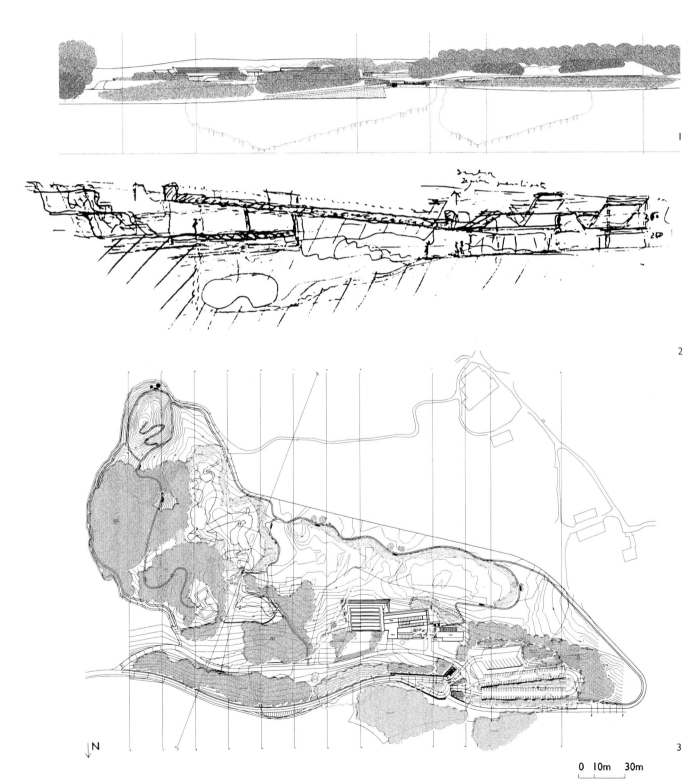

1

2

↓N

3

0   10m   30m

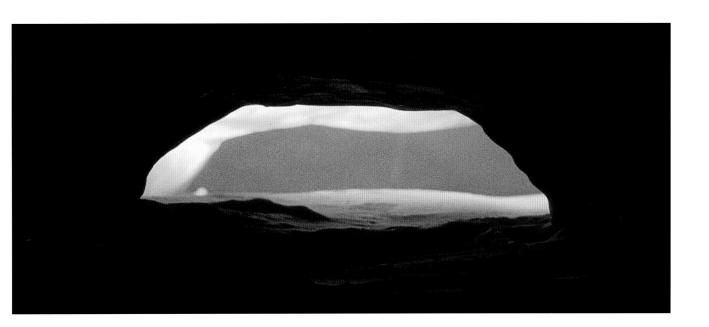

With these objectives in mind, the site for the museum and the new research center was selected west of the cave, on the opposite slope of the hill on which it is located, and separated from it by abundant vegetation. The site lent itself well for the integration of the new construction into the slope, which descends towards the north, and made it possible to endow the entry to the new cave with an orientation similar to that of the original cave. Furthermore, the site fell outside the drainage area of the cave, avoiding any possible alteration on this account.

The museum, the cave replica, and the research center were divided into two differentiated wings, of which one houses the replica and the other consists of a series of volumes that extend linearly from the common vestibule. These volumes, which are arranged almost parallel to one another, have a primary structure composed of large beams and a secondary structure of sheeting that opens and rises towards the north in order to facilitate the introduction of light into the exhibition areas. Several open-air terraces are situated on the structure's western end. The desire to integrate the new construction into the landscape was at odds with the large roof area required to cover the replica. In order to overcome this conflict, the design proposed the construction of a roof that follows the natural slope of the land – a roof that is covered with grass and incorporates a system of linear skylights. The research center, the laboratory area, and the director and administration offices have all been housed in the intermediate space between the new cave and the roof in order to incorporate them into the same area as the museum.

1 Exhibition hall wing
2 Cross section through the exhibition halls
and lecture rooms
3 Permanent collection exhibition hall

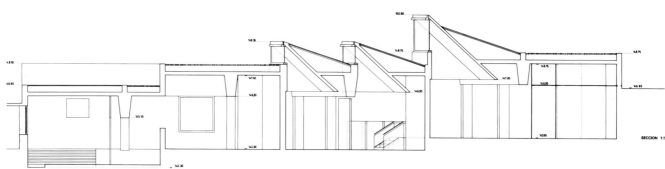

SECCION 1:1

0   1m   3m

1 Detail of the library structure above the cave replica

2 Section through the cave replica

3 View of the cave replica suspended from the roof structure

1

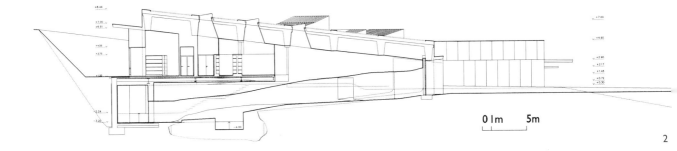

2

0 1m   5m

1 South elevation
2 North elevation
3 West elevation
4 Floor plan, level -1.00 to +1.55
5 View from the north
6 View from the south

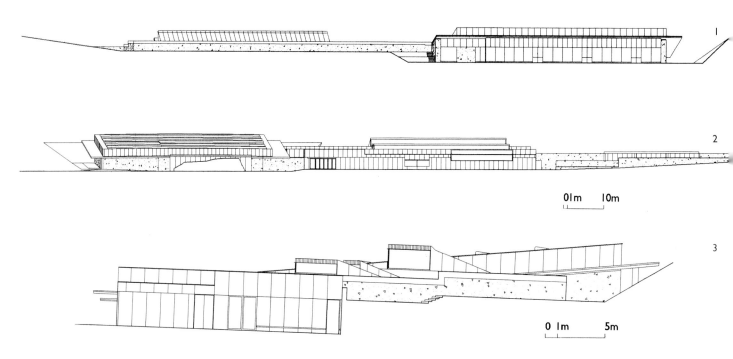

01m   10m

0 1m   5m

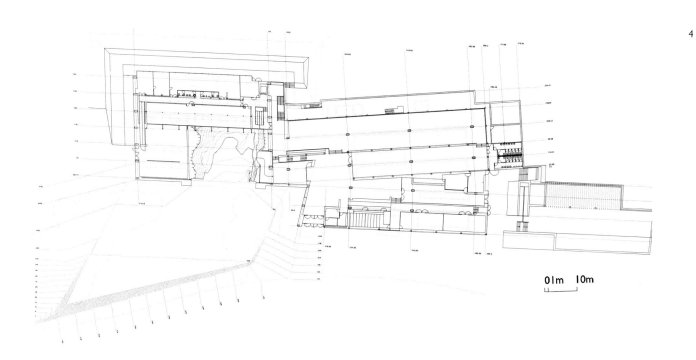

01m   10m

DEVELOPER Altamira Consortium: Spanish Ministry of Education and Culture, Marcelino Botín Foundation, Cantabria Regional Council, Santillana del Mar Town Hall, Spanish Ministry of Economy and Treasury
STRUCTURAL CALCULATIONS MC-2, Julio Martínez Calzón
CONSTRUCTION COMPANY NECSO Entrecanales y Cubiertas, S.A

Benidorm Cultural Center

Benidorm. Alicante. Spain
1997-1999

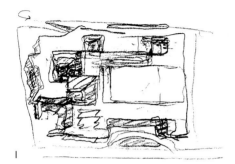

1

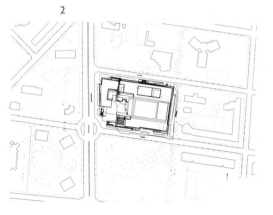

2

1 Preliminary sketch

2 Area map

3 Model of the lobby and the entry to the
   convention hall

Benidorm's Cultural Center has been designed to spread out over an entire city block using an architecture that is organized around a series of patios. The proposal presents this block as a regular volume whose constant height is only broken by that of the auditorium, which rises to the required height of 27 meters. The compact character of the design thus fills the site in the city's expansion area, the *ensanche*, in a manner that differs radically from the typical architecture of Benidorm, which mostly consists of freestanding high-rise buildings with gardens. It is precisely through this differentiated treatment of the site that the Center expresses its singular character in the city.

Benidorm's mild climate suggests that the patios will be used as open-air gathering spaces and lobbies for public acts and intermissions during conventions. The variable degree of intimacy of these patios makes them appropriate for a variety of different activities. At the same time, there is a clear awareness of the importance of the roof, visible from the nearby high-rises, which will be treated as a façade that can be viewed from above.

The courtyard on the corner of Europa Avenue and Ibiza Street, conceived as a reception patio of white-glazed brick, leads to other more intimate courtyards of ocher and blue brick. Additional patios on the upper floor correspond to the School of Dance and Music, with walls of pink and ocher brick respectively. This complex of patios is organized and linked three-dimensionally in space, climbing and cutting into the compact volume of the building. The figure of these courtyards, carved into the volume and decked with plants, enables us to designate the roof as a "roof garden".

The proposal combines and regulates the dependence or independence of the Center's activities according to the changing and organic desires of use. The independence of the different functions is assured by differentiated entries, which permit individual control of each type of activity.

The main entrance to the auditorium is located on Ibiza Street, although it can also be reached from the patio on the corner of Europa Avenue and Ibiza Street. The library and museum are accessed from the central patio. The School of Dance and Music is entered from Jaén Street, as well as from the interior of the auditorium area. The workshops are reached from the corner of Jaén Street and Europa Avenue. Loading and unloading for the auditorium takes place from Jaén Street; and for the museum, from Ibiza Street.

One of the aspects of the project that was developed with great precision, both conceptually and formally, is the way in which light penetrates the large auditorium and the lobbies. Skylight is introduced through "pillows of light" formed by opal glass walls. As a result, the volume of the acoustic ceiling appears to float like a fabric in a translucent curvilinear perimeter. In this way, the hall and the lobbies are endowed with a special luminous atmosphere and are animated by a singular illusory effect.

The entire body of the Cultural Center building expresses its character as a network, in which the constitutive elements manifest, in their continuity, the form of a fabric of uninterrupted planes.

1 South elevation

2 Cross section

3 Longitudinal section through the main hall

4 Sketch

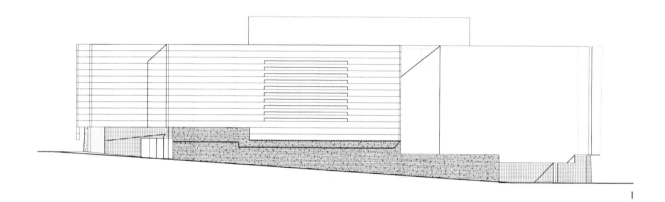

1

2

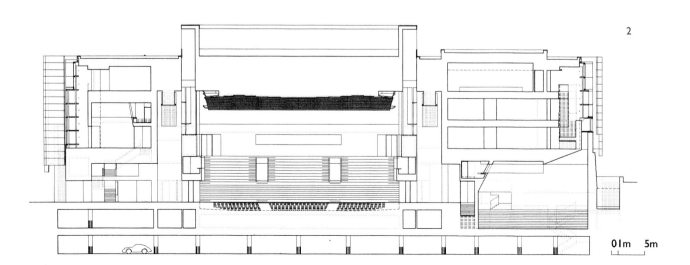

01m   5m

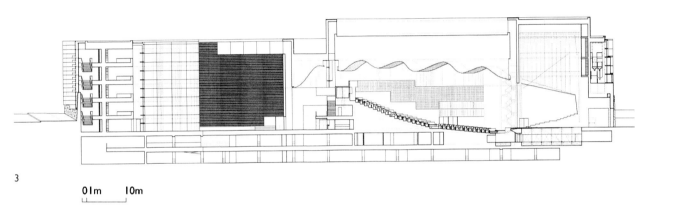

3

01m   10m

4

1 Floor plan, level +7.56
2 Floor plan, level +15.48
3 Competition model
4 Cross section through the library

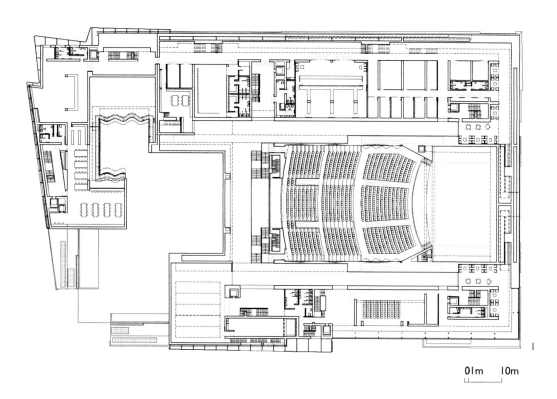

01m   10m

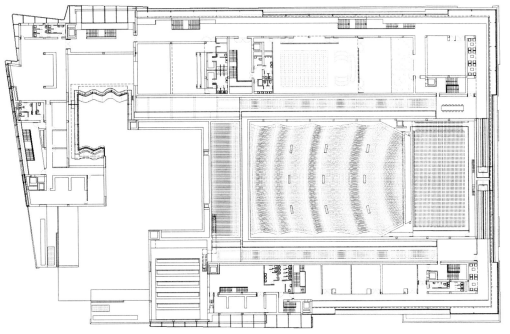

3

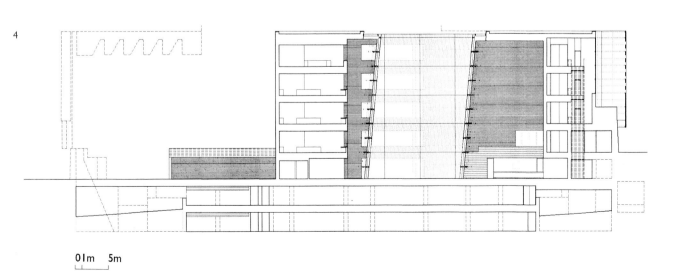

4

0 1m   5m

1 Pillows of light. Partial cross section of the
construction
2 Pillows of light. Partial cross section of the
proscenium
3 Model. Staircase to the convention hall

1

DEVELOPER Benidorm Town Hall and Autonomous
Community of Valencia
STRUCTURAL CALCULATIONS Proyectos de Ingeniería y
Arquitectura, S.L. (José M. Fernández Álvarez)

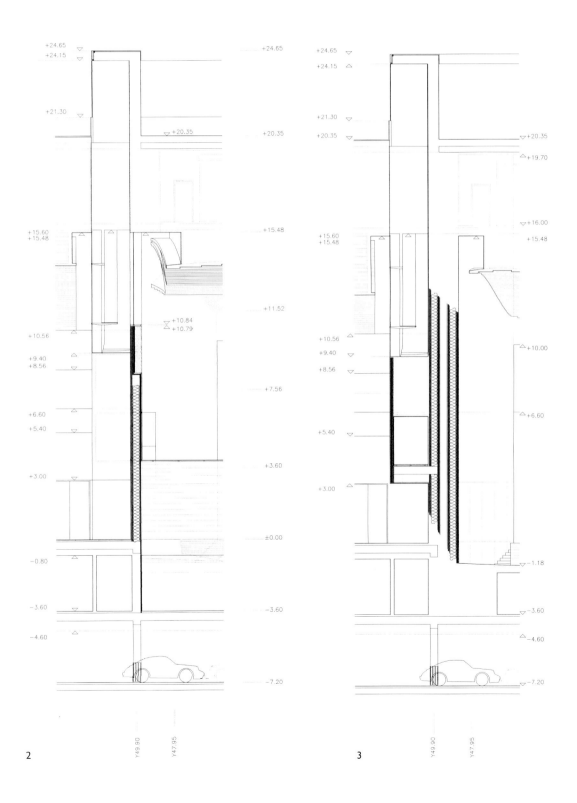

2

3

University of Las Palmas Law, Business and Economics Campus

University of Las Palmas de Gran Canaria
1991, 1993-96, 1994-98, 1995-99

The design for the Law, Business and Economics area of the university campus in Tafira established an integrated layout of buildings articulated around a common open area. The need to create a coherent urban nucleus in this part of the campus required careful consideration of the scale of the built modules, the fragmentation of the program, and the definition of volumes, and lead to the treatment of the common open space as a pleasant meeting and strolling area. The buildings were thus made to fit in well with the concentric horizons present on the site.

The ensemble consists of lecture room buildings common to all faculties, departmental buildings for the Law School and the School of Business and Economics, a general library, an auditorium, and a small administration building. These volumes form a line that follows the axis marked by the curved paths for car and pedestrian traffic.

The program was developed following organic criteria, fragmenting the brief into free-standing or almost free-standing buildings designed to minimize the impact of a large mass on the surroundings and to avoid the monotonous layout of a single, linear volume on the elongated site. The separate units were designed to endow the ensemble with the right scale needed to create a formally varied exterior, made up of differentiated places, capable of offering a wealth of situations, experiences and viewpoints to its users. Large corridors were avoided whenever possible, while lobbies, common interior areas, ramps, and halls were given generous dimensions in order to enhance their value. The varied exterior appearance of the different volumes was made to reflect the uses of each building – the façades of the departmental buildings are governed by a repetitive division of discrete window openings; the lecture room buildings are characterized

1 Area map

2 Law School departmental buildings

N
→

Common lecture room building

1 View from the departmental buildings

2 Southeast elevation

3 Cross section through the lecture rooms

4 Cross section through the ramps

1

by continuous bands of horizontal windows protected by a system of *brise-soleils*. This dual system of fenestration was repeated in the buildings to unify their formal appearance and facilitate the transparency and legibility of their functions.

The progam of the common lecture room building was housed in two modules located in the western part of the campus and placed in a slightly skewed alignment. The axis of the ensuing broken line marks an access and communication path between the two volumes. The staircase placed here responds to the change in grade between two open areas. The two modules of the lecture room building are communicated at ground floor level, facilitating an alternated use of these wings, i.e. in an integrated or separated fashion, depending on the needs of the moment. This enveloping gesture helps to delimit a large open-air area.

The School of Business and Economics program was also divided into two modules. These two buildings are positioned in a line following the curvature of the general site plan.

As in the case of the common lecture room building, their functional division responds to the general criterion dictating the fragmenting of the program of the schools into units with precise scales.

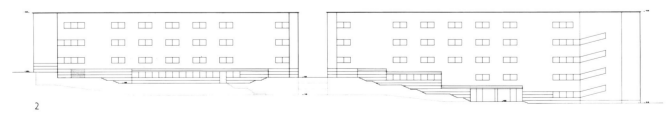

2

0 1m   10m

The criteria used in the design of the Law School were similar to those followed when designing the School of Business and Economics. The program was divided between two buildings that house departmental offices and complementary lecture rooms. The modules have "U" and "H"-shaped ground plans whose geometry responds to the need to fragment and condition the perimeter of the site. The compositional system of discreet window openings and continuous bands of window openings shaded with canopies and *brise-soleils* is similar to that of the other buildings in the Legal and Economic Sciences area.

The central buildings are made up of a large auditorium, a common library and an administrative building. These three volumes house the most representative functions of the area and therefore occupy a preeminent position in the ensemble. The fan-shaped form of the auditorium and the star-shaped form of the library help to establish a flexible arrangement of volumes in the most pronounced curve of the general site plan, thus solving the contact and continuity with the schools that extend on both sides. Their geometric definition establishes a link between modules and creates a centralized and precise image from the distance.

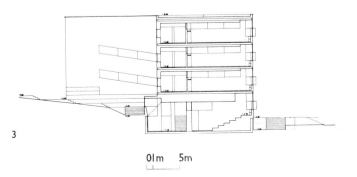

3

0 1m   5m

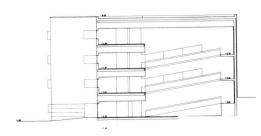

4

1 General floor plan
2 Interior view of the entry to the Law School departmental building
3 Interior view of the ramp in the Law School

N →

2

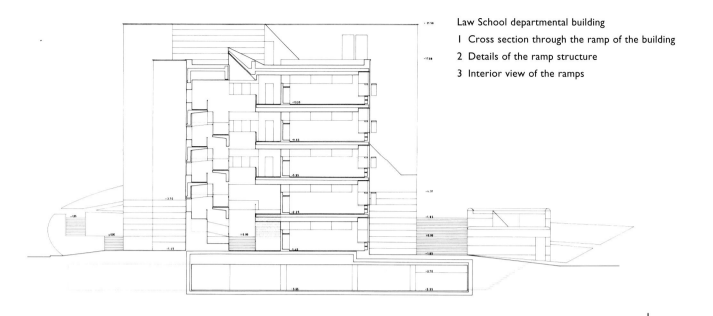

Law School departmental building

1 Cross section through the ramp of the building
2 Details of the ramp structure
3 Interior view of the ramps

1

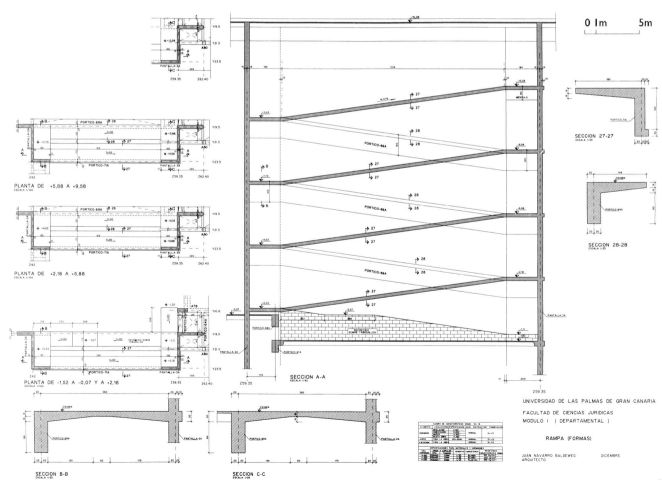

2

School of Business and Economics

1 Front elevation

2 Lecture room floor plan, elevation, and
section

3 Detail of the south façade

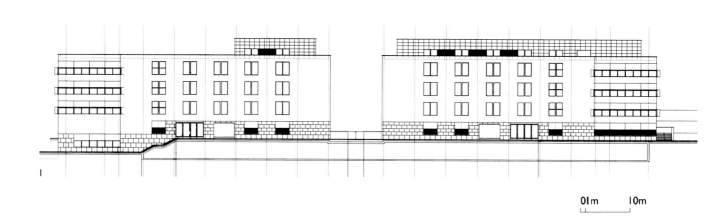

1

01m 10m

2

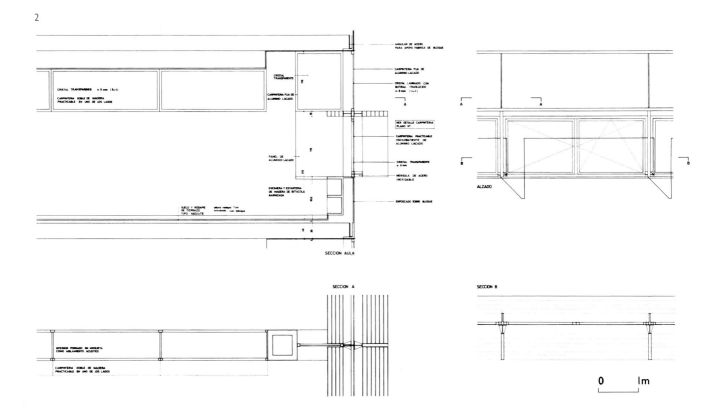

1 Detail of lecture room *brise-soleils*
2 Norheast façade of the common lecture room building
3 Detail of lecture room *brise-soleils* according to different orientations
4 Detail of the windows of the School of Business and Economics departmental building

2

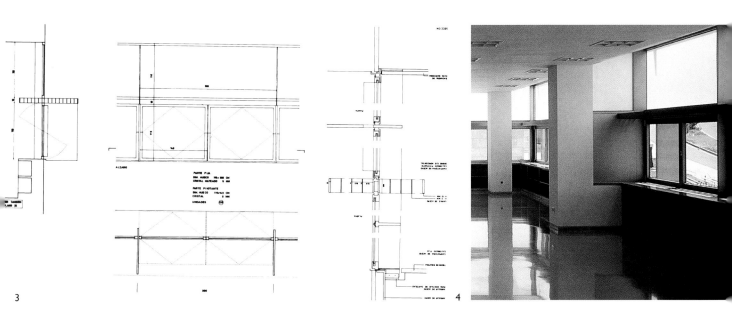

3

4

Works and Projects

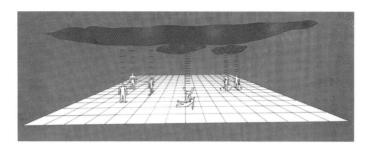

Informational Architecture
"Sounding Mirror"
1970
A light-sound transducer that creates
a sounding environment responsive to
people's spatial configurations

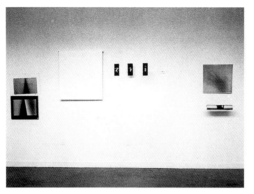

"Shadow Pieces"
1973

Bibliography: 18, 99, 100

House for an Intersection
1976
Competition design

Bibliography: 13, 18, 33, 39, 41, 42, 72, 76, 78,
94, 95, 103, 109, 119, 140

"Interior VI"
1978
Installation at the Venice Biennial

Bibliography: 18, 78, 94, 95

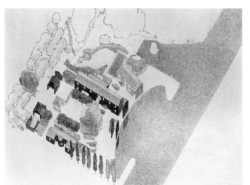

House for Karl Friedrich Schinkel
1979
Competition design

Bibliography: 13, 41, 42, 82, 94, 95, 119

House of Rain
Single Family Residence
Alto la Hermosa, Santander, Spain
1978

Bibliography: 13, 18, 29, 32, 37, 39, 41, 42, 70, 71, 72, 78, 82, 94, 95, 96, 97, 99, 100, 103, 109, 110, 112, 115, 119, 127, 131, 132, 138, 140, 146, 147, 148, 149, 150, 151, 152, 153, 154, 155, 158, 159, 160, 161, 165, 173, 179

Twelve Houses in Calpe
1980
Design

Bibliography: 94, 95

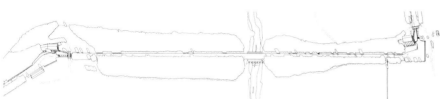

Rehabilitation of the Castilla Canal
1981
Design

Bibliography: 18, 78, 94, 95

EL RIO MANZANARES EN MADRID

Manzanares River Park
Madrid, Spain
1981
Design

Bibliography: 94, 95

San Francisco el Grande
Urban Distribution Plan
Madrid, Spain
1982
Design

Bibliography: 13, 18, 30, 37, 41, 42, 60, 61, 62, 78, 86, 94, 95, 99, 100, 103, 115, 122, 126, 131, 132, 133, 139, 179, 192

Social Services Center
Puerta de Toledo, Madrid, Spain
1982-1989

Bibliography: 13, 26, 28, 30, 40, 41, 42, 50, 57,
59, 61, 62, 69, 85, 86, 94, 95, 96, 97, 99, 100, 110,
119, 121, 122, 128, 131, 132, 133, 138, 139, 146,
147, 148, 149, 150, 151, 152, 153, 154, 155, 158,
159, 160, 161, 191, 192

Rehabilitation of the Segura River Mills for a Hydraulics Museum and Cultural Center
Murcia, Spain
1984-1988

Bibliography: 3, 13, 27, 28, 37, 41, 42, 53, 57, 59,
69, 70, 71, 82, 94, 95, 96, 97, 99, 100, 103, 105,
109, 113, 115, 116, 119, 121, 122, 124, 131, 132,
133, 134, 139, 142, 145, 146, 147, 148, 149, 150,
151, 152, 153, 154, 155, 158, 159, 160, 161, 179,
183, 188, 191

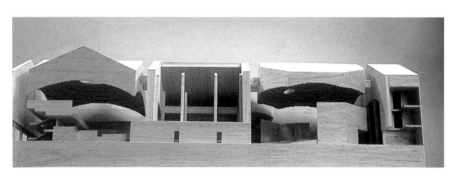

Santander Festival Hall
1984
Competition design

Bibliography: 13, 37, 94, 95, 96, 97, 103, 109,
112, 119, 125, 179, 183, 191

Intervention in Alto Belo
1984
Design

Bibliography: 94, 95

"Domestic Hydraulics"
1985
Installation for the Milan Triennial

Bibliography: 18, 78, 94, 95, 110, 119, 138

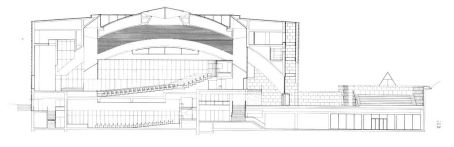

Castilla y León Convention Center and Exhibition Hall
Salamanca, Spain
1985-1992

Bibliography: 2, 7, 13, 18, 28, 31, 36, 37, 39, 41, 42, 54, 55, 56, 57, 59, 67, 69, 70, 71, 77, 78, 82, 83, 86, 92, 93, 94, 95, 96, 97, 99, 100, 102, 103, 105, 108, 109, 110, 112, 119, 121, 123, 125, 128, 131, 132, 133, 138, 142, 145, 146- 155, 158, 159, 162, 163, 170, 172, 183, 185, 189, 191

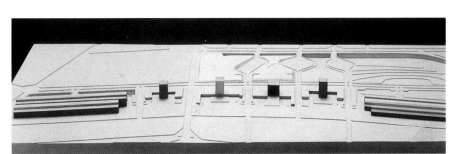

Urban Rehabilitation Project for Turin
1986
Milan Triennial
Design

Bibliography: 13, 58, 82, 94, 95, 109, 119, 142, 175, 176, 183

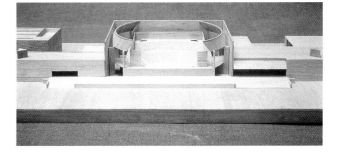

Cádiz Convention Center and Exhibition Hall
1988
Competition design

Bibliography: 13, 28, 57, 70, 71, 78, 82, 94, 95, 109, 119, 191

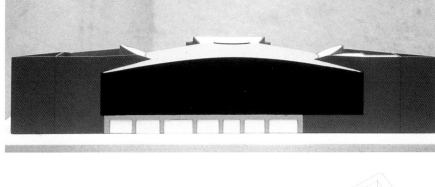

Olympic Village Training Pavilion in Barcelona
1988
Competition design

Bibliography: 13, 49, 70, 71, 82, 94, 95, 109, 119, 142, 191

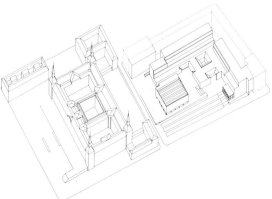

Ministry of Defense Cultural Center
Madrid, Spain
1988
Competition design

Bibliography: 94, 95

Regional Government of Extremadura Presidential Offices and Administrative Buildings
Mérida, Spain
1989-1995

Bibliography: 9, 13, 41, 42, 51, 69, 82, 92 (photo),
94, 95, 99, 100, 101, 103, 112, 119, 120, 121, 128,
131, 132, 142, 146, 147, 148, 149, 150, 151, 152,
153, 154, 155, 169, 170

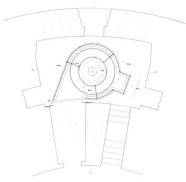

Installation for the "Architecture and Imagination" Exhibition
Fort Asperen, United States
1989

Bibliography: 77, 94, 95, 99, 100, 109, 142

Auditorium
San Sebastián Convention Center
and Exhibition Hall
San Sebastián, Spain
1990
Competition design

Bibliography: 13, 94, 95, 99, 100

Pedro Salinas Public Library
Puerta de Toledo
Madrid, Spain
1990-1994

Bibliography: 2, 8, 13, 15, 17, 30, 40, 41, 42, 50,
52, 59, 61, 62, 63, 82, 85, 86, 96, 97, 99, 100, 103,
105, 107, 110, 112, 131, 132, 142, 146, 147, 148,
149, 150, 151, 152, 153, 154, 155, 158, 159, 164,
183, 189

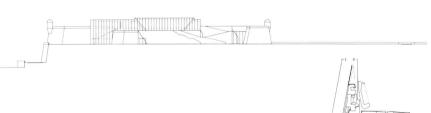

Sant Pere Bastion
Palma de Mallorca, Spain
1991
Competition design

Bibliography: 94, 95

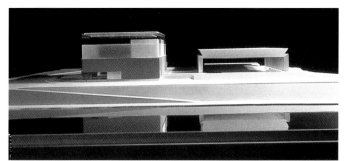

Center for the Performing Arts
Blois, France
1991
Competition design

Bibliography: 13, 94, 95, 99, 100, 103, 112, 119, 142, 191

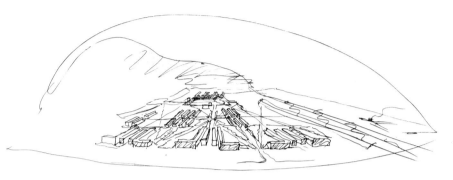

Urban Rehabilitation Project for the Nordbahnhofgelände
Vienna, Austria
1991
Design

Bibliography: 13, 94, 95, 119

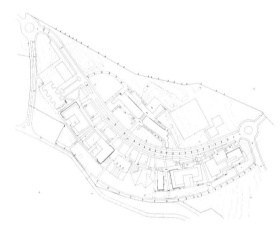

Law School and Schools of Business and Economics
University of Las Palmas de Gran Canaria
Tafira, Spain
1991, 1993-96, 1994-98, 1995-99
Work in progress in other phases

Bibliography: 99, 100, 146, 147, 148, 149, 150, 151, 152, 153, 154, 155

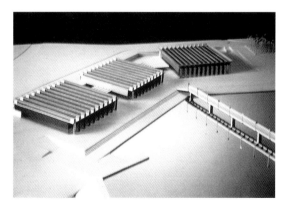

Silleda Trade Fair Grounds
Pontevedra, Spain
1992
Competition design

Bibliography: 13, 82, 94, 95, 99, 100, 119, 142, 191

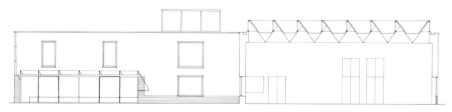

Painter's House and Studio
Villanueva de la Cañada, Madrid, Spain
1992
Design

Bibliography: 94, 95, 119, 142, 191

Convention Center
Salzburg, Austria
1992
Competition design
First Prize

Bibliography: 41, 42, 82, 87, 92, 94, 95, 99, 100, 120, 142, 146, 147, 148, 149, 150, 151, 152, 153, 154, 155

Cultural Center
Villanueva de la Cañada, Madrid, Spain
1992-1997

Bibliography: 11, 44, 45, 46, 47, 48, 49, 82, 92, 94, 95, 99, 100, 103, 105, 120, 120.1, 131, 132, 142, 146, 147, 148, 149, 150, 151, 152, 153, 154, 155, 158, 159, 170, 177, 191

New Courthouse
Mahón, Minorca, Spain
1992-1996

Bibliography: 10, 22, 82, 92, 94, 95, 99, 100, 105, 103, 120, 146, 147, 148, 149, 150, 151, 152, 153, 154, 155, 158, 159, 167, 168, 170

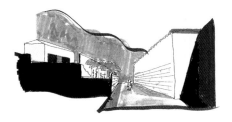

Proposal for the Getty Museum Expansion
Malibu, United States
1993
Competition

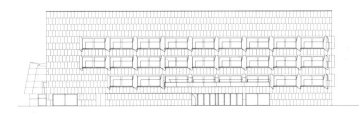

Department of Industry and Tourism
Toledo, Spain
1993
Design

Bibliography: 94, 95, 99, 100, 120

Salvador Allende Museum and Cultural Center
Santiago de Chile, Chile
1993
Competition design

Bibliography: 41, 42, 82, 89, 94, 95, 99, 100, 103, 117, 120, 146, 147, 148, 149, 150, 151, 152, 153, 154, 155, 191

Single-family House
Alicante
1993

Bibliography: 99

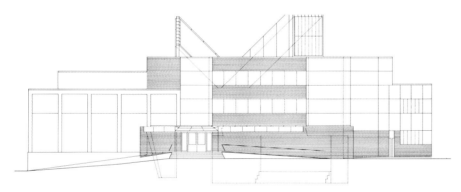

Woolworth Center of Music Addition
Princeton University
Princeton, New Jersey, United States
1994-1997

Bibliography: 6, 12, 16, 31, 41, 42, 82, 90, 94, 95, 99, 100, 103, 105, 106, 111, 120, 129, 146, 147, 148, 149, 150, 151, 152, 153, 154, 155, 170, 187

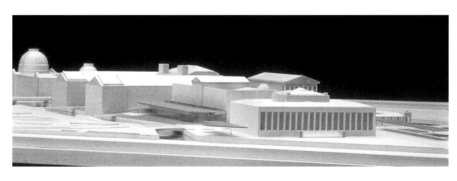

Museum Island
Berlin, Germany
1994
Restricted competition design

Bibliography: 94, 95, 99, 100, 120, 142

Altamira Museum & Research Center
Santillana del Mar, Cantabria, Spain
1994-2000

Bibliography: 4, 41, 42, 68.1, 82, 91, 93.1, 94, 95, 98, 99, 100, 120, 158, 159, 164.1, 166, 170, 177.1

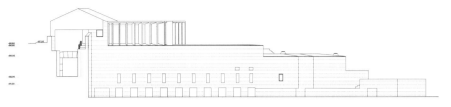

Urban Development of "Molino de Martos y Rivera del Estadio"
Córdoba, Spain
1994
Draft design

Bibliography: 94, 95, 184

Theater
Salamanca, Spain
1995
Design

Bibliography: 94, 95

Hertziana Library
Rome, Italy
1995
Restricted competition design

Bibliography: 5, 41, 42, 82, 92, 94, 95, 130, 146, 147, 148, 149, 150, 151, 152, 153, 154, 155

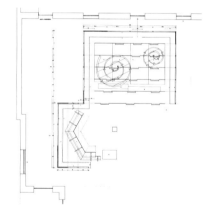

Installation for the Milan Triennial
1995

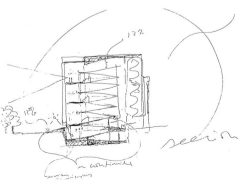

Departamental Building and Lecture Room Building in Ciutadella
Pompeu Fabra University
Barcelona, Spain
1996
Competition design

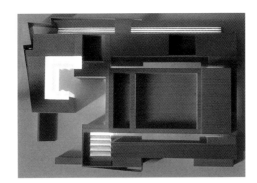

Cultural Center
Benidorm, Spain
1997 / 1999
Design

Residential Development and Underground Parking in Paseo Doña Dolores Piera
Benissa, Alicante, Spain
1997

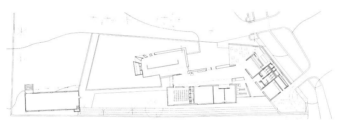

Haría House and Museum
Taro de Tahiche, Lanzarote, Spain
1998
Preliminary study and design

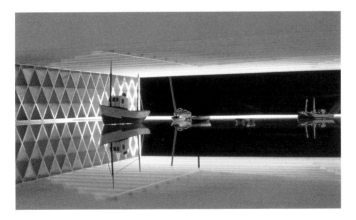

Preliminary Ideas for the Arrecife Marina Project
Lanzarote, Spain
1998

Bibliography: 76, 82, 105

Galician City of Culture
Santiago de Compostela, Spain
1999
Competition

Bibliography: 190

Reina Sofía National Museum of Art Expansion
Madrid, Spain
1999
Competition design

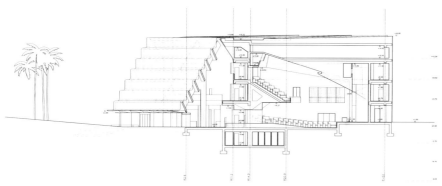

Aula Magna Hall, Library and Administration Building for the Law, Business and Economics Campus
University of Las Palmas de Gran Canaria
2000
Draft design

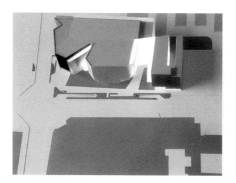

Center for the Performing Arts, Canal Theater
Madrid
July 2000
Competition design

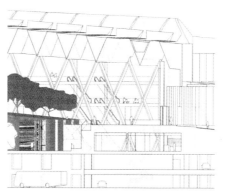

Restricted-entry International Competition for the "Solar de Caballería", Museum of Human Evolution
Burgos
September 2000
Competition design

1939 Juan Navarro Baldeweg is born in Santander, Spain.

1959-60 He studies Engraving at the Escuela de Bellas Artes de San Fernando, Madrid, Spain.

1960-65 He studies Architecture at the Escuela Técnica de Arquitectura de Madrid, Spain.

1969 He obtains his PhD. in Architecture at the Escuela Técnica Superior de Arquitectura de Madrid, Spain.

1970 As a scholar of the Fundación Juan March, he studies abroad.

Juan Navarro Baldeweg
Oria 13
28002 Madrid, Spain
Tel. 34 91 562 68 01, Fax 34 91 562 16 51
E mail   jnbaldeweg@arquired.es

Academic Experience

1971-75 Guest researcher, invited by Professor Gyorgy Kepes, at the Center for Advanced Visual Studies, Massachusetts Institute of Technology, Boston, Massachusetts, USA.

1977 Professor of Design at the Escuela Técnica Superior de Arquitectura de Madrid, Spain.

1987 Guest lecturer at the School of Architecture of Pennsylvania University, Philadephia, Pennsylvania, USA.

1990 Guest lecturer at the School of Architecture of Yale University, Eero Saarinen Professor, New Haven, CT, USA.

1992 Guest lecturer at the School of Architecture of Princeton University, Jean Labatut Professor, Princeton, New Jersey, USA.

1997 Guest lecturer at the Graduate School of Design, Harvard University, Kenzo Tange Professor, Princeton, Cambridge, MA, USA.

2000 Guest lecturer, "Architecture, Criticism and Design" postgraduate course, La caja de resonancia workshop, Escuela Técnica Superior de Arquitectura del Vallés, Barcelona.
Guest lecturer, "Architectural Design" postgraduate course, Escuela de Arquitectura, University of Navarre, Pamplona.

Awards

1978 Guest artist at the Spanish Pavilion for the Venice Biennial.
First prize in the competition for a Single Family Residence in Madrid organized by the Madrid Architects' Chamber.

1979 First prize in the international competition for A House for Friedrich Schinkel, The Schinkenchiku Residential Design Competition. Judge: James Stirling.

1982 First prize in the competition of ideas for the Urban Layout of the San Francisco el Grande area, organized by the Madrid City Council.

1985 First prize in the competition of ideas for the Castilla y León Convention Center and Exhibition Hall in Salamanca.

1986 Guest participant at the *Il Progetto Domestico: La Casa dell'Uomo, Archetipi e Prototipi* exhibition in the XVII Milan Triennial.

1988 First prize in the competition of ideas for the Olympic Village Training Pavilion in Barcelona.
First prize in the competition of ideas for the Cádiz Convention Center and Exhibition Hall.
Autonomous Region of Murcia Architecture and Town Planning Award for the Segura River Mills Cultural Center and Hydraulics Museum, Murcia.

1989 First prize in the competition of proposals for the Regional Government of Extremadura Presidential Offices and Administra-tive Buildings in Mérida.

1990 National Plastic Arts Award.

1991, 1992 Finalist, Mies van der Rohe Prize.

1992 First prize in the international competition for the Salzburg Convention Center, Austria.

1993 First prize in the restricted competition for the Salvador Allende Museum, Santiago de Chile.
Madrid City Council New Architecture Award for the Pedro Salinas Municipal Library, Madrid.
Cámara de Contratistas de Castilla y León Award for the Castilla y León Convention Center and Exhibition Hall in Salamanca.
Architecture of Stone international award, Inter-marmomach Veronafiere, Verona, for the Castilla y León Convention Center in Salamanca.

1994 Dragados y Construcciones Architecture Award for the Castilla y León Convention Center and Exhibition Hall in Salamanca.

1995 First prize in the restricted competition for the Remodelling of the Hertziana Library, Max-Planck-Gesellschaft, Rome.

1996 First prize in the competition of ideas for the Construction of a Departmental and Lecture Room Building in the Area of Ciutadella for the Pompeu Fabra University in Barcelona.

1997 First prize in the competition for the design of the Benidorm Cultural Center.

1998 Heinrich Tessenow Gold Medal.
Finalist in the Mies van der Rohe Prize.

2000 First prize in the restricted competition for the Canal Theater, Madrid.
First prize in the competition for the "Solar de Caballería", Burgos (Museum of Human Evolution).
Homage, Arquitectura y Patrimonio FIL 2000, Guadalajara, Jalisco, Mexico.

Individual Exhibitions

1960 Fernando Fe Gallery, Madrid, Spain.

1965 Edurne Gallery, Madrid, Spain.

1972 Massachusetts College of Art, Boston, Massachusetts, USA.

1975 Carpenter Center, Harvard University, Cambridge, Massachusetts, USA. *Projects, Environments, Installations*, Center for Advanced Visual Studies, Cambridge, Massachusetts, USA.

1976 *Luz y Metales*, Vinçon Gallery, Barcelona.
La Habitación Vacante, Buades Gallery, Madrid, Spain.

1978 *Pinturas 1962-65*, Buades Gallery, Madrid, Spain.
Interior VI, Spanish Pavilion, Venice Biennial, Italy.

1980 *Pinturas y Piezas 1979-80*, Buades Gallery, Madrid, Spain.

1982 *Pinturas 1980-82*, Juana de Aizpuru Gallery, Seville, Spain.
Eco y Narcisos, Pinturas 1981-82, Galleriet. Lund, Sweden.

1983 *Pinturas 1980-83*, Ciento Gallery, Barcelona, Spain.
Pinturas 1982-83, Ariadne Gallery, Vienna, Austria.
Pinturas 1983, Juana de Aizpuru Gallery, Madrid, Spain.

1984 *Pinturas 1983*, Miguel Marcos Gallery, Zaragoza, Spain.

1985 *Pinturas*, Casa de Goya Cultural Center, Bordeaux, France.
Pinturas, Juana de Aizpuru Gallery, Seville, Spain.

1986 *Pinturas*, Italiana Gallery, Alicante, Spain.
Pinturas 1980-86, Museo Español de Arte Contemporáneo (catalog), Madrid, Spain / Museo de Bellas Artes, Santander, Spain.
Pinturas, Miguel Marcos Gallery, Zaragoza, Spain.

1987 *Pinturas*, Palacete-Embarcadero, Santander, Spain.
Pinturas, Ciento Gallery, Barcelona, Spain.

1988 *Pinturas*, Temple Gallery, Valencia, Spain.

1989 *Pinturas*, Chamber of Commerce, Santander, Spain.

1990 *Pinturas*, Juana de Aizpuru Gallery, Madrid, Spain.

1991 *Paisajes*, Juana de Aizpuru Gallery, Seville, Spain.
Pinturas, Málaga Architects' Chamber, Spain.

1992 *Pinturas*, Córdoba Architects' Chamber (catalog), Córdoba, Spain.
Juan Navarro Baldeweg, Banco Zaragozano, (catalog), Zaragoza, Spain.
Pinturas, Fernando Silió Gallery, Santander, Spain.

1994 *Pinturas*, Juana Aizpuru Gallery, Madrid, Spain.
Architecture, Paintings and Pieces, Arge Kunst Gallery, Bolzano, Italy.
Architecture, Paintings and Pieces, DeSingel Gallery, Antwerp, Belgium.

1995 *Architecture, Paintings and Pieces*, ETH Exhibition Hall, Zürich, Switzerland.
Architecture, Paintings and Pieces, ETH Exhibition Hall, Lausanne, Switzerland.
Juan Navarro Baldeweg, Senda Gallery, Barcelona, Spain.

1996 *Historia Natural*, 1995-96 works, Juana de Aizpuru Gallery, Seville, Spain.

1997 *Complementary Geometry*, Graduate School of Design, Harvard University, Cambridge, USA.
Historia Natural, 1995-96 works, Juana de Aizpuru Gallery, Madrid, Spain.
Juan Navarro Baldeweg, Arquitectura, Piezas y Pintura, Fundación Marcelino Botín, Santander.
Juan Navarro Baldeweg, travelling exhibition, Santillana del Mar, Cantabria, Pamplona, and Logroño, Spain.

1998 *Juan Navarro Baldeweg*, Luis Adelantado Gallery, Valencia, Spain.
Arquitectura, Piezas y Pintura, Juan Navarro Baldeweg, Architect's Chamber of Catalonia, Girona Division, Spain.
Juan Navarro Baldeweg, Festspielhaus Hellerau, Desden, Germany.

1999 *Juan Navarro Baldeweg, Architektur + Kunst*, Renate Kammer Gallery, Hamburg, Germany.
Juan Navarro Baldeweg, Luis Adelantado Gallery, Valencia, Spain.
Juan Navarro Baldeweg, Senda Gallery, Barcelona, Spain.
Juan Navarro Baldeweg, IVAM Centre del Carme, Valencia, Spain.

2000 *La caja de resonancia, pintura reciente*, Marlborough Gallery, Madrid, Spain.
John Soane, Architetto 1753-1837, Juan Navarro Baldeweg, Rissonanze di Soane, Andrea Palladio International Centre for Architectural Studies, Palazzo Barbaran da Porto, Vicenza, Italy.

Collective Exhibitions

1972 *Encuentros en Pamplona*, Pamplona, Spain.

1973 *MIT Travelling Show*, Chicago, Cincinnati, New Orleans, Philadelphia, and New York, USA.
CAYC, *Hacia un Perfil del Arte Latinoamericano*, Buenos Aires, Argentina.

1974 *Asterisk*, Lobby 7, Massachusetts Institute of Technology, Cambridge, Massachusetts, USA.
To John Cage, Concert Design, Kirkland House, Harvard University, Cambridge, Massachusetts.

1975 Projects Inc. *Videotapes* (together with Ernst Caramelle), Cambridge, Massachusetts, USA.

1977 *VII Encuentro Internacional de Video*, Fundación Joan Miró, Barcelona, Spain / Caja de Ahorros de Alicante, Spain / Alexander Iolas Gallery, New York, USA.

1978 Nachst St. Stephan Gallery, Vienna, Austria.

1979 *Contemporary Spanish Prints*, travelling exhibition across the USA.

1980 *Madrid D.F.* Municipal Museum, Madrid, Spain.

1981 *4 PM*, Fúcares Gallery, Almagro, Ciudad Real / Leyendecker Gallery, Santa Cruz de Tenerife, Spain.

Ocho Pintores de Madrid, Pamplona City Council, Pamplona, Spain.
Forma y Color, Theo Gallery, Madrid, Spain.

1982 *Cinco Pintores y un Escultor*, Foro Cívico Cultural Pozuelo, Madrid, Spain.
Arco'82, International Art Fair in Madrid, Grupo 15 and Juana Aizpuru Gallery stands (with Carlos Alcolea and Aguirre).
26 Pintores y 13 Críticos, La Caixa de Pensiones de Barcelona Cultural Center, Barcelona, Valencia and Madrid, Spain.
Libro de Artistas, Sala Picasso, Dirección General de Bellas Artes de Madrid, Spain.
Preliminar, Ist National Biennial of Plastic Arts, Zaragoza, Spain.

1983 *Homenaje a Murillo*, Juana de Aizpuru Gallery, Seville, Spain.
Cuadernos de Viaje, Fundación Miró, Barcelona.
Accrochege, Fúcares Gallery, Almagro, Spain.
Seventh Art Biennial, Pontevedra, Spain.
Art '83 Basle, Basle, Switzerland, Juana de Aizpuru Gallery stand.
Cologne International Fair, Juana de Aizpuru stand.
Spansk Egen-Art, Liljevalchs Konsthall, Stockholm, Sweden.

1984 *Arco'84*, International Art Fair in Madrid, Spain.
Ariadne Gallery, Vienna, Austria.
Salón de los 16, Madrid, Spain.
Artistas de la Galería, Juana de Aizpuru Gallery, Madrid, Spain.
Temple Gallery, Valencia, Spain.
Chisel Gallery, Italy.

1985 *Cota-Cero*, Alicante, Seville, Madrid, and Valencia, Spain.
Art'85 Basle, Basle, Switzerland, Juana de Aizpuru Gallery stand.
Chicago International Art Fair, Juana de Aizpuru Gallery stand.
Milano Internacional d'Arte Contemporáneo, Juana de Aizpuru Gallery stand.
Pontevedra Biennial, Spain.
Sao Paulo Biennial, Sao Paulo, Brazil.
The Nude, Juana de Aizpuru Gallery, Madrid, Spain.

1986 *Milan Triennial*, Milan, Italy.
17 Artistas 17 Autonomías, Pabellón Mudéjar, Seville / La Lonja, Palma de Mallorca, Spain.
Arco'86, Juana de Aizpuru Gallery stand, Madrid, Spain.
Chicago International Art Fair, Juana de Aizpuru Gallery stand.
Art'86 Basle, Basle, Switzerland, Juana de Aizpuru Gallery stand.
Pintores-Arquitectos, E.T.S. School of Architecture, Barcelona, Spain.
A Mi Perro, J. de Aizpuru Gallery, Madrid, Spain.
Sketch de la Nueva Pîntura (homage to García Lorca), Palacio de los Condes de Gabia, Granada, Spain.
Pintores y Arquitectos, Málaga Architects' Chamber, Málaga, Spain.
Pintores de Cantabria, Palacio de San Rafael, Asamblea Regional de Cantabria, Santander, Spain.

1987 La Caixa Cultural Center, Barcelona, Spain.
Proyecto para una Colección, Galería Juana de Aizpuru Gallery, Madrid, Spain.
Naturalezas Españolas, 1940-1987, Centro Nacional de Arte Reina Sofía, Madrid, Spain.

1988 *Muestras de Artistas Españoles*, European Parliament, Strassburg / Palazzo della Triennale, Milan, Italy.
Arco'88, Juana de Aizpuru stand, Madrid, Spain.
Salón de los 16, MEAC, Madrid, Spain.
Alfons Roig y sus Amigos, Sala Parpalló, Valencia, Spain.
El Retrato, Juana de Aizpuru Gallery, Madrid, Spain.
Los Angeles Art Fair, California, Juana de Aizpuru Gallery stand.

1989 *Colección Testimonio*, La Caixa, Barcelona, Spain.
Arco'89, Juana de Aizpuru Gallery stand, Madrid, Spain.
Los Angeles Art Fair, California, Juana de Aizpuru Gallery stand.
Antes y Después del Entusiasmo, ART RAI-89, Amsterdam, The Netherlands.
Luz y Metales installation by Navarro Baldeweg.

1990 *About Round. Round About*, Anders Tornberg Gallery, Lund, Sweden.

1991 *23 Artistas. Madrid Años 70*, Comunidad de Madrid Exhibition Hall / Mie Prefectual Art Museum, Japan / Exhibition Hall, Hashin, Japan.

1992 *Building in a New Spain* (architecture exhibition) Art Institute of Chicago, Chicago, USA.

1994 *Museos y Arquitectura, Nuevas Perspectivas*, Círculo de Bellas Artes, Madrid, Spain.
Itinere. Camiño e Camiñante, Centro Galego de Arte Contemporànea, Santiago de Compostela, Galicia, Spain (December).

1995 *Itinere. Camiño e Camiñante*, Centro Galego de Arte Contemporànea, Santiago de Compostela, Galicia, Spain (January and February).
A la Pintura. Pintores Españoles de los Años 80 y 90 en la Colección Argentaria, Palau de la Virreina, Barcelona, Spain.

1996 *Identità e differenze. Integrazione e pluralità nelle forme del nostro tempo. Le culture tra effimero e duraturo* international exhibition at the XIX Milan Triennial, Milan, Italy.
Cinco Premios Nacionales de Artes Plásticas, PS Gallery, Burgos, Spain.
Estampa 96, Taller Antonio Gallo Ediciones stand, Madrid, Spain.

1997 *45 x 28*, Senda Gallery, Barcelona, Spain.
"La casa, su idea", in *Ejemplos de la Escultura Reciente*, Comunidad de Madrid, Madrid, Spain.
Arco'97, International Art Fair, Juana de Aizpuru Gallery, Madrid / Senda Gallery, Barcelona / Luis Adelantado Gallery, Valencia, Spain.
Una Mirada Tensa, Marlborough Gallery, Madrid, Spain.
Pintura y Obra Gráfica Luis Gordillo, Juan Navarro Baldeweg, Centro Cultural La Despernada, Villanueva de la Cañada, Madrid, Spain.

FIA'97, Luis Adelantado Gallery, Venezuela.
Paisajes de un Siglo, Centro Cultural Casa del Cordón, Burgos, Spain.

1998 *Tomás Seral. Un Galerista en la Posguerra*, Centro Cultural Conde Duque, Madrid / Salas de la Corona de Aragón, Hermanos Bayeu and María Moliner in Zaragoza, Spain.
Dibujos Germinales, Museo Nacional Centro de Arte Reina Sofía, Madrid, Spain.

1999 *Imágenes de la Abstracción 1969-1989*, Sala de las Alhajas, Fundación Caja de Madrid / Salas Julio González y Manuel Millares, Museo Español de Arte Contemporáneo, Madrid, Spain.
Arco'99, International Art Fair, Madrid, Spain.
De Buena Tinta, graphic works, VII Estampa Fair, Madrid, Spain.

2000 *Arco'00*, International Art Fair, Luis Adelantado Gallery stand, Valencia / Senda Gallery stand, Barcelona, Spain.
Viaje a la semilla, Provincial Muesum, Teruel, Spain.
Ideas sobre el concepto. Aproximación a la escultura española actual, Sala de Armas de la Ciudadela, Pamplona, Spain.

2001 *Arco'01*, International Art Fair, Madrid, Spain.

Texts by Juan Navarro Baldeweg

"Una casa para Karl Friedrich Skinkel," "Movimiento ante el ojo. Movimiento del ojo," "Notas acerca de las figuras de una lámina," "Doce viviendas en Calpe," "Una mesa," and "El Canal de Castilla", *Arquitectura*, no. 234, Madrid, 1982.

"Proyecto para la ordenación de San Francisco el Grande," *Arquitectura*, no. 239, Madrid, 1982.

"Concurso para el Palacio de Festivales de Santander," *Arquitectura*, no. 250, Madrid, 1984.

"Concurso en Salamanca. Anteproyectos para el concurso para la construcción del Palacio y Sala de Conciertos, Exposiciones, Convenciones y Sala de Conciertos de Castilla y León," *Arquitectura*, no. 225, Madrid, 1985.

"La Puerta de Toledo," *Arquitectura*, no. 260, Madrid, 1986.

"Amanegements des abords de la Porte de Toledo" and "Palais des Congres. Salamanca," *L'Architecture d'Aujourd'hui*, Paris, 1986.

"Lungo il canale di Castiglia. Un precorso attraverso i manufatti," *Lotus International*, no. 52, Milan, 1987.

"Alejandro de la Sota," catalog, Harvard University Graduate School of Design, USA, 1987.

"Centro de Servicios Sociales Puerta de Toledo" and "Centro Cultural de los Molinos del Río Segura," *Arquitectura*, no. 271-272, Madrid, 1988.

"A forza dunha imaxe," *Grial*, no. 109, Spain, 1991.

"Complementary Geometry," *Lotus International*, no. 73, Milan, 1992.

"Nordbahnhofgelände," *Wiener Architektur-Seminar*, Vienna, 1992.

"The Convention and Exhibition Center of Salamanca: An object is a section: The project," *Perspecta 27*, The Yale Architectural Journal, USA, 1992.

Juan Navarro Baldeweg, Conference and publication, Agre Kunst Gallery, Bolzano, Italy, 1994.

"Del silencio a la luz," *A&V Monografías de Arquitectura y Vivienda*, no. 44, Madrid, 1994.

"Desde la Academia," *Accademia Spagnola di Storia, Archeologia e Belle Arti*, Rome, Italy, 1996.

"Sobre la litografía," in Juan Navarro Baldeweg, *Noche*, catalog published by Estiarte Gallery, Madrid, 1996.

"Construir, habitar: los dibujos de Alejandro de la Sota para la urbanización de Alcudia," *A&V Monografía Alejandro de la Sota*, no. 68, Madrid, 1997.

"El acuerdo entre la mano y la mirada," first published under the title of "Alvar Aalto – Die Übereinstimmung Zwischen Hand und Blick," *Alvar Aalto Gesellschatf*, Bulletin 8, Germany, 1998.

"Figuras de luz en la luz," *Lotus*, no. 98, Electa, Milan, 1998.

"Libre de servidumbres," text for the catalog of the Alvaro Siza exhibition held at the Fundación ICO, Madrid, 1998.

"Libero de asservimenti," *Alvaro Siza,* in *Scultura Architettura*, Brescia Mostre, Skira, Milan, 1999.

"Light and Gravity," *John Soane, Architect: Master of Space and Light*, London, 1999.

"Biblioteca Hertziana, Max-Planck-Institut, Roma," *Building for Science, Architecture of the Max Planck Institutes*, Birkhäuser, Basle, 1999.

La habitación vacante, Pre-Textos de Arquitectura, Valencia, 1999.

"Figuras de luz en la luz," *Bia arquiterctura,* nº 7, Valencia, 2000.

"A Resonance Chamber", *Assemblage,* no. 41, Cambridge, Massachusetts, 2000.

"Edifici per l'Università," Las Palmas de Gran Canaria", *Casabella*, no. 679, Milan, 2000.

"Museo y Centro de Investigación Altamira," *a+t,* no. 16, Vitoria, 2001.

"Museo e centro studi. Cave di Altamira," *Casabella*, no. 687, Milan, 2001.

"El museo de la evolución en Burgos," *Anuario 2000. Diario de Burgos*, Burgos, 2001.

Bibliography

[1]. Álvarez Reyes, J. A. *Algunas ideas e imágenes con forma de casas,* 1997.

[2]. Arcidi, P. "The Substance of Light." *Progressive Architecture*, May 1994.

[3]. — "Hydraulics Museum, Murcia, Spain / Juan Navarro Baldeweg." *Progressive Architecture,* no. 5, May 1990.

[4]. Arquitectura Viva. "Navarro en Altamira, el original y su réplica." *Arquitectura Viva*, no. 40, Madrid, 1995.

[5]. — "Una biblioteca de Navarro en Roma." *Arquitectura Viva*, no. 48, Madrid, 1996.

[6]. — "Navarro Baldeweg, de estreno en Princeton." *Arquitectura Viva,* no. 57, Madrid, 1997.

[7]. A & V Monografías. "Palacio de Congresos, Salamanca." Anuario, Madrid, 1993.

[8]. — "Biblioteca Puerta de Toledo." *A & V Monografías*, no. 45–46, Madrid, 1994.

[9]. — "Sede de la Junta de Extremadura, Mérida." *A & V Monografías*, no. 57–58, Madrid, 1996.

[10]. — "Juzgados de Mahón (Menorca)." *A & V Monografías*, no. 63–64, Madrid, 1997.

[11]. — "Centro Cultural, Villanueva de la Cañada." *A & V Monografías*, no. 69–70, Madrid, 1998.

[12]. — "Pasaje cultural. Biblioteca del Centro de Música Woolworth, Princeton." *A & V Monografías*, no. 63, Madrid, 1999.

[13]. Baldellou, M. A.; Capitel, A. " *Summa Artis: Historia general del Arte. XL: Arquitectura española del siglo XX*. Madrid: Espasa Calpe, 1995.

[14]. Benevolo, L. *Historia de la Arquitectura Moderna*. Seventh edition. Barcelona, Gili, 1994.

[15]. "Biblioteca Puerta de Toledo." *Kenchiku Bunka*, vol. 50, no. 580, Tokyo, 1995.

[16]. "Bibliotecas. Ampliación y Biblioteca del Centro Woolworth de Música." *On Diseño,* no. 199, Barcelona, 1999.

[17]. Bienal de Arquitectura Española. Selection Committee: Peña Ganchegui, L.; Solá-Morales, I. de; Fernández-Galiano, L.; Kleihues, J. P.; Coquhoum, A.; Grassi, G.; Waisman, M.; Buchanan, P. R.; Benet, J. (International Jury). *I Bienal de Arquitectura Española. 1991*. Madrid: MOPTMA, CSCAE, UIMP, 1991."Biblioteca Puerta de Toledo, Madrid." Madrid: MOPT, 1993.

[18]. Bonet, J. M. "Pistas para una biografía." Juan Navarro Baldeweg exhibition at the Museo Español de Arte Contemporáneo. Madrid, 1986.

[19]. — "Juan Navarro Baldeweg." *Studio International*, no. 7, Madrid, 1984.

[20]. — *Juan Navarro Baldeweg, 26 pintores, 13 críticos*. Barcelona: La Caixa, 1982.

[21]. — *Fuente y fuga: Mapa*. Catalog. Madrid: Galería Buades, 1980.

[22]. Bravo, I. "Nuevos Juzgados en Mahón." *Diseño Interior*, no. 58, Madrid, 1996.

[23]. Brea, J. L.; Navarro Baldeweg, J. "La conversación de Leonardo." *Antes y después del entusiasmo*, Amsterdam, 1989.

[24]. — "Tras el concepto, escepticismo y pasión." *Comercial de la Pintura*, no. 2, Madrid, 1983.

[25]. Buchanan, P. "Invisibly anchored and complex plays of light fill the buildings by Spanish architect Juan Navarro Baldeweg." *Architecture*, USA, October 1997.

[26]. — "Palazzo and Acropolis, Rafael Moneo, Juan Navarro Baldeweg." *The Architectural Review*, no. 1115, London, 1990.

[27]. — "Murcia Metaphors." *The Architectural Review*, no. 1120, London, 1990.

[28]. — "Tras la década dorada. El desafío de los noventa." *A + V*, no. 24, Madrid, 1990.

[29]. — "A través del cristal. Una casa de Juan Navarro Baldeweg." *A + V*, Madrid, 1988.

[30]. — "Above the Gate." *The Architectural Review*, no. 1084, London, 1987.

[31]. Buchner, A.; Rosenow, C. "Verleihung der Tessenow-Medaille an Juan Navarro Baldeweg." *Stadt Bauwelt*, no. 139, Berlin, 1998.

[32]. Bulnes, P. *Figuras de definición*. Madrid: F. Rivas Ediciones, 1980.

[33]. — *La habitación vacante. Luz y metales*. Barcelona: Sala Vinçon / Madrid: Galería Buades, 1976.

[34]. Calvo Serraller, F. *Geografía y Sueño*. Catalog. Juan Navarro Baldeweg exhibition at the Pabellón de Mixtos, Ciudadela, Pamplona, October 1997.

[35]. Cameron, D. "Report from Spain." *Art in America*, 1985.

[36]. Capitel, A. "Bóveda, templo e idea en el Palacio de Congresos de Salamanca." *Diseño Interior*, no. 18, Madrid, 1992.

[37]. — *Arquitectura española, años 50 – años 80*. Madrid: Dir. Gral. Arquitectura, MOPU, 1986.

[38]. Capitel, A.; Solá-Morales, I de. *Contemporary Spanish Architecture. An Eclectic Panorama*. New York: Rizzoli, 1986.

[39]. Capitel, A.; Mateo, J. L; Pérez Escolano, V.; Fullaondo, J. D. *et al. Architecture Espagnole: Trente oeuvres. Années 50 – années 80*. Europalia catalog. Madrid: MOPU, 1985.

[40]. Capitel, A. et al. *Arquitectura de Madrid, siglo XX*. Madrid: Tanais Ediciones / Fundación Antonio Camuñas, 1999.

[41]. — *Arquitectura del siglo XX: España*. Madrid: Tanais Ediciones / Sociedad Estatal Hanover 2000, Seville / Madrid, 2000.

[42]. — *Twentieth-Century Architecture: Spain*. Madrid: Tanais Ediciones / Sociedad Estatal Hanover 2000, Seville / Madrid, 2000.

[43]. Castro, M. A. de. "Estancias y paisajes." *Diseño Interior*, no. 18, Madrid, 1992.

[44]. "Centro Cultural en Madrid: una lección ejemplar de composición." *Diseño Interior*, no. 64, Madrid, 1997.

[45]. "Centro Cultural en Villanueva de la Cañada: la gratificante dificultad de conseguir la sencillez." *Bia*, no. 189, Madrid, 1997.

[46]. "Centro Cultural en Villanueva de la Cañada." *On Diseño*, no. 183, Barcelona, 1997.

[47]. "Centro Cultural en Villanueva de la Cañada. Juan Navarro Baldeweg." *Diseño Interior*, no. 64, Madrid, 1997.

[48]. "Centro Cultural en Villanueva de la Cañada. Juan Navarro Baldeweg." *Dialogue*, no. 10, Taipei, Taiwan, 1997.

[49]. "Centro Sportivo. Juan Navarro Baldeweg." *Lotus International*, no. 67, Milan, 1990.

[50]. Cohn, D. "Die Regenerierung der Stadt. Sozialzentrum und Bibliothek an der Puerta de Toledo, Madrid." *Bauwelt*, no. 27, Berlin, 1995.

[51]. — "Sobrevolando la historia. Consejerías de la Junta de Extremadura, Mérida." *Arquitectura Viva*, no. 44, Madrid, 1995.

[52]. — "Neue Bibliotheken in Spanien." *Deutsche Bauzeitung*, no. 5, May 1994.

[53]. Croset, P. A. "Un 'restauro' esemplare di Juan Navarro Baldeweg a Murcia." *Casabella*, no. 552, Milan, December 1988.

[54]. Curtis, W. J. R. *Modern Architecture since 1900*. London: Phaidon, 1996.

[55]. — "El monumento y la ciudad." *L'Architecture d'Aujourd'hui*, no. 283, Paris, 1992.

[56]. — "Paisaje, ciudad y sustitución" (Castilla y León Convention Center and Exhibition Hall in Salamanca). *Archithese*, no. 5, Zurich, 1991.

[57]. — "Una perspectiva histórica. España durante los ochenta." *A + V*, no. 24, Madrid, 1990.

[58]. De Rossi, P. *Progettare nella citta*. Milan: Umberto Allemandi, 1988.

[59]. Dossier "Juan Navarro Baldeweg." *L'Architecture d'Aujourd'hui*, no. 283, Paris, 1992.

[60]. Ezquiaga, J. M. "L'area di San Francisco el Grande a Madrid: un progetto per punti." *Casabella*, no. 526, Milan, 1986.

[61]. — "La esquina ausente: Navarro Baldeweg en la Puerta de Toledo." *Arquitectura Viva*, no. 3, Madrid, November 1988.

[62]. — "El proyecto urbano como reinterpretación de la ciudad." San Francisco el Grande competition: Social Services Center and Library designs, Puerta de Toledo, Madrid) *Archithese*, no. 5, Zurich, 1991.

[63]. Feduchi, P. "Navarro Baldeweg. Un universo lleno de referencias." *Diseño Interior*, no. 38, Madrid, 1994.

[64]. Fernández, B. "Juan Navarro Baldeweg; el espacio y la luz." *RS*, no. 7, Madrid, 1991.

[65]. Fernández-Cid, M. "Juan Navarro Baldeweg." *Artistas en Madrid*, 1992.

[66]. Fernández-Galiano, L. "Cinco estrellas: formas de la sociedad-opulencia," *Arquitectura Viva*, no. 51–52, Madrid, 1995.

[67]. — "Un dosel de luz: Palacio de Congresos, Salamanca." *Arquitectura Viva*, no. 51–52, Madrid, 1995.

[68]. — "Septiembre: mes de piedra." *Arquitectura Viva*, no. 57–58, Madrid, 1996.

[68.1]. — "La sima luminosa." *Babelia, El País* cultural supplement, Madrid, 10 March 2001.

[69]. Flores, C.; Güell, X. *Guía Arquitectura de España 1929-1996*. Barcelona: Fundación Caja de Arquitectos, 1996.

[70]. Frampton, K.; Capitel, A.; Pérez Escolano, V.; Solá-Morales, I. de. *Building in a New Spain*. Chicago – Barcelona: The Art Institute – Gili, 1992.

[71]. — *España: Arquitecturas de hoy*. Madrid: MOPT, 1992.

[72]. Frechilla, J. "Juan Navarro Baldeweg. El Arte ante la Arquitectura, el Arte de la Arquitectura." *Arquitectura*, no. 234, Madrid, 1982.

[73]. García, A. "Un edén doméstico." *Figura*, Seville, 1985.

[74]. — "Juan Navarro Baldeweg." *Artforum*, New York, 1984.

[75]. García-Herrera, A. "Los premios." *Arquitectura Viva*, no. 75–76, Madrid, 1999.

[76]. González García, A. "Todo lo verdadero es invisible." IVAM Exhibition, Valencia, 1999.

[77]. — "Conversación con Juan Navarro Baldeweg: el espacio y sus sinergias." *El Paseante*, no. 18–19, Madrid, 1991.

[78]. — *Pinturas. Juan Navarro Baldeweg*. Madrid: Museo Español de Arte Contemporáneo, 1986.

[79]. — "Juan Navarro Baldeweg." *17 Artistas, 17 Autonomías* exhibition catalog. 1986.

[80]. — "El método del ladrón de tumbas." Catalog. Barcelona: Galería Ciento, 1983.

[81]. — "Juan Navarro Baldeweg." *Comercial de la Pintura*, no. 2, Madrid, 1983.

[82]. Granell Trias, E. "Una caja de botones en un cruce de caminos." Juan Navarro Baldeweg at the IVAM , Valencia, 1999.

[83]. — "El nuevo auditorio de Salamanca." *Figura*, Seville, 1985.

[84]. Guasch, A. "Tres opcions plástiques: Navarro Baldeweg, Amat i Pere-Jaume." *L'ull sobre les Arts*, Barcelona, November 1987.

[85]. Guerra de la Vega, R. "Guía de Madrid no. 3." *Nueva Arquitectura*, author's edition, Madrid, undated.

[86]. Guolet, P. "Temps sauvage et incertain." *L'Architecture d'Aujourd'hui*, no. 245, Paris, 1986.

[86.1]. Hernández León, J. M. "Juan Navarro. Los espacios narrados." interview with Juan Navarro Baldeweg, *Pasajes de arquitectura y crítica*, no. 25, Madrid, 2001.

[87]. Hollein, H. "Il concorso per il nuovo Palazzo di Congressi di Salisburgo." *Zodiac*, no. 10, Milan, 1993.

[89]. Isasi, J. "El blanco espacio del arte: un museo de Navarro Baldeweg en Santiago de Chile." *Arquitectura Viva*, no. 38, Madrid, 1994.

[90]. Kraft, B. "Erweiterungsbau des Woolworth Musikzentrums, Princeton, Strukturell aufgefaßt." *DBZ-Deutsche Bauzeitschrift*, no. 2, Gütersloh, 1999.

[91]. Lahuerta, J. J. "Juan Navarro Baldeweg. The Altamira Cave Museum, Santillana del Mar, since 1995." *Museums for a New Millennium, Concepts, Projects, Buildings*. Munich: Prestel, 1999.

[92]. — "Le belle pietre." *Casabella*, no. 639, Milan, November 1996.

[93]. — "Palacio de Congresos, Salamanca." *Domus*, no. 745, Milan, 1992.

[93.1]. — "Il museo della grotta di Altamira, avvero l'architettura di Narciso." *Casabella*, no. 687, Milan, 2001.

[94]. Lahuerta, J. J.; González García, A. *Juan Navarro Baldeweg. Opere e Progetti*. Milan: Electa, 1990.

[95]. — *Juan Navarro Baldeweg; Obras y Proyectos*. Madrid: Electa, 1992.

[96]. Lampugnani, Vittorio Magnano (ed). *Hatje / Lexikon der Architektur des 20. Jahrhunderts*. Ostfildern-Ruit: Verlag Gerd Hatje, 1998.

[97]. — *Enciclopedia de la Arquitectura del siglo XX*. Barcelona: Gili, 1989.

[98]. Lasheras, J. A. "Il Museo di Altamira." *Lotus*, no. 103, Milan, 1999.

[99]. Lupano, M. *Juan Navarro Baldeweg – Il ritorno della luce*. Milan: Federico Motta, 1996.

[100]. — *Juan Navarro Baldeweg – Die Rückkehr des Lichts*. Basel: Wiese Verlag, 1996.

[101]. — "L'inaudita congunzione fra un ponte di Santiago Calatrava e un'architettura di Juan Navarro Baldeweg." *Lotus*, no. 90, Milan,1996.

[102]. — "El ejercicio del espacio complementario." Juan Navarro Baldeweg in Salamanca. *Lotus International*, no. 74, Milan, 1992.

[103]. Malagamba, D. "Die latenten Strukturen eines Ortes." *DBZ-Deutsche Bauzeitschrift*, no. 9–99, Gütersloh, 1999.

[104]. Marchan Fiz, S. "La deconstrucción moderna de la cabaña primitiva." *La Casa, su Idea*. Madrid: Consejería de Educación y Cultura, Comunidad de Madrid, 1997.

[105]. — "Convivencia entre las artes. Juan Navarro Baldeweg expone en el IVAM." *Arquitectura Viva*, no. 65, Madrid, 1999.

[106]. Marpillero, S. "Maschere tettoniche. Tectonic Masks." Navarro Baldeweg, Woolworth Center of Music, Princeton University. *Lotus*, no. 99, Electa, Milan, 1999.

[107]. Martorell, C. "Biblioteca en la Puerta de Toledo, una cúpula flotante." *Diseño Interior*, no. 38, Madrid, 1994.

[108]. — "Un pulso con gravedad." *Diseño Interior*, no. 18, Madrid, 1992.

[109]. Mata, S. de la; Nieto, F.; and Sobejano, E. "Entrevista a Juan Navarro Baldeweg." *Arquitectura*, no. 274, Madrid, 1988.

[110]. Melis, Liesbeht. "Klassieken opnieuw geïnterpreteed." *De Architect*, no. 23, Gravenhage, 1992.

[111]. Méndez, R. "Music Box, Music Library, Princeton." *The Architectural Review*, no. 1226, London, April.

[112]. Mik, E. "Interview with Juan Navarro Baldeweg." *Archidea*, Amsterdam, Autumn 1993.

[113]. "Molinos del Río Segura." *Bordes Urbanos II*. Cuadernos de la Dirección General de Arquitectura y Edificación. Madrid: MOPT, 1986.

[114]. Montaner, J. M. *Nuevos Museos. Espacios para el arte y la cultura*. Barcelona, Gili, 1990.

[115]. Muñoz, M. T. "Entrevista a Juan Navarro Baldeweg." *Periferia*, no. 1, Seville, 1984.

[116]. "Museum und Kulturzentrum los Molinos in Murcia." *Detail*, no. 3, Munich, 1989.

[117]. *Museos y Arquitectura: nuevas perspectivas*. Catalog. Madrid: MOPTMA, 1994.

[118]. Navarro Baldeweg, J. (see page 189).

[119]. — "Juan Navarro Baldeweg." Monograph. *El Croquis*, no. 54, Madrid, 1992.

[120]. — "Juan Navarro Baldeweg." Monograph. *El Croquis*, no. 73 II, Madrid, 1995.

[120.1]. — "Juan Navarro Baldeweg. Centro culturale a Villanueva de la Cañada. Antiretorica della forma e retorica della luce." *Casabella*, no. 655, Milan, 1998.

[121]. Nicolin, P. "La bellezza vaga." *Domus*, no. 775, Milan, 1995.

[122]. — "Trascrizioni." *Lotus International*, no. 58, Milan, 1988.

[123]. Ontiveros, A. "Bajo una cúpula flotante." *Cercha*, no. 38, Madrid.

[124]. Ortelli, L. "Somiglianze e differenze." *Lotus International*, no. 59, Milan, 1988.

[125]. — "Luoghi della città." *Lotus International*, no. 48–49, Milan, 1985.

[126]. — "Puntuale e puntiforme. Un progetto di Juan Navarro Baldeweg." *Lotus International*, no. 39, Milan, 1983.

[127]. Pieltain, A. "Juan Navarro Baldeweg, Casa de la Lluvia, Liérganes (Santander) 1978–1982." *Arquitectura Viva*, no. 60, Madrid, 1996.

[128]. Pisapia, P. *Dieci anni di architettura spagnola, 1987-1996*. Milan: Electa, 1998.

[129]. Pitzalis, E. "Juan Navarro Baldeweg, Woolworth Music Center, Princeton." *Area*, no. 46, Milan, 1999.

[130]. — "Juan Navarro Baldeweg. Biblioteca Hertziana a Roma." *Area*, no. 30, Milan, 1997.

[131]. Pizza, A. *Guida all'architettura del Novecento. Spagna*. Milan: Electa, 1997.

[132]. — *Guía de Arquitectura del novecientos. España*. Madrid: Electa, 1997.

[133]. Poisay, C. "Pintor y arquitecto." *L'Architecture d'Aujourd'hui*, no. 283, Paris, 1992.

[134]. Pousse, J. F. "Coeur de ville. Musée Hidraulique del río Segura. Murcie. Espagne." *Techniques Arquitecture*, no. 387, Paris, 1989.

[135]. Power, K. "Una canción medida. Juan Navarro Baldeweg." Catalog of the Navarro Baldeweg exhibition held at the Palacete-Embarcadero, Santander, 1987.

[136]. — "Juan Navarro Baldeweg. Colores de la Cultura." *Figura*, Seville, 1985.

[137]. — "Conversaciones con Juan Navarro Baldeweg." *Conversaciones con Miguel Barceló, José Manuel Broto, Miguel Angel Campano, Gerardo Delgado, Ferrán García Sevilla, Juan Navarro Baldeweg, Guillermo Pérez Villalta y Manolo Quejido*. Alicante, 1985.

[138]. Quetglas, J. Definición de arquitectura." *Figura*, Seville, 1985.

[139]. — "Sobre Juan Navarro Baldeweg." *Arquitectura*, no. 271–272, Madrid, 1988.

[140]. — "Paysage au miroir." *A 30*, no. 5, Barcelona, November 1986.

[141]. — "Juan Navarro Baldeweg, obras y proyectos." *Arquitectura Viva*, no. 33, Madrid, 1993.

[142]. — "4 – 10 – 4 – 5." *Juan Navarro Baldeweg*. Bolzano: Arge Kunst Gallery, 1994.

[143]. Rabat, E. "Juan Navarro Baldeweg y la Ciento." *Arts Plástiques*, Barcelona, 19 November 1987.

[144]. Reindl, U. "Juan Navarro Baldeweg." *Kunstforum*, vol. 94, 1988.

[145]. Richardson, M. "Soane's Legacy." *John Soane, Architect: Master of Space and Light*. London: Royal Academy of Arts, 1999.

[146]. Rispa, R. (Ed.), Solá-Morales, I. de, et al. *Guía de Arquitectura. España 1920–2000*. Seville: Tanais Ediciones, 1998. Book format version of the *Registro de Arquitectura de España, fase 1920–2000 register*, Ministerio de Fomento, Tanais Ediciones.

[147]. — *Architectural Guide. Spain 1920–1999*. New York: Birkhäuser, 1998.

[148]. — *Architecture Guide. Spain 1920–2000.* Seville: Tanais, 1998.

[149]. — *Guida d'architettura. Spagna 1920–2000.* Modena: Logos, 1998.

[150]. — *Guida d'architettura. Spagna 1920–2000.* Seville: Tanais, 1998.

[151]. — *Architekturführer. Spanien 1920–1999.* Basel: Birkhäuser, 1998.

[152]. — *Architekturführer. Spanien 1920–2000.* Seville: Tanais, 1998.

[153]. — *Architectuurgids. Spanje 1920–2000.* Bussum: Thoth, 1999.

[154]. — *Architectuurgids. Spanje 1920–2000.* Seville: Tanais, 1999.

[155]. — Guide d'architecture. Espagne *1920–2000.* Seville: Tanais, 2001.

[156]. Rivas, F. "Algunas cosas que he aprendido viendo pasear a Juan Navarro Baldeweg por la calle de Serrano (a contramano)." Catalog. Madrid: Salón de los 16, 1988.

[157]. Rubio, P. "Entrevista con Juan Navarro Baldeweg." *Lápiz*, Madrid, 1986.

[158]. Ruiz Cabrero, G. *El Moderno en España: Arquitectura después de 1940.* Seville: Tanais, 2001.

[159]. — *The Modern in Spain: Architecture after 1948.* Cambridge: MIT Press, 2001.

[160]. — *Spagna: Architettura 1965–1988.* Milan: Electa 1989.

[161]. — *España: Arquitectura 1965–1988.* Madrid: Electa, 1989.

[162]. Sainz, J. "La cúpula ingrávida. Palacio de Congresos, Salamanca." *Arquitectura Viva*, no. 24, Madrid, 1990.

[163]. — "Ingravidez simbólica. Juan Navarro en Salamanca." *Arquitectura Viva*, no. 25, Madrid, 1992.

[164]. — "El tambor de hojalata. Juan Navarro, una biblioteca en Madrid." *Arquitectura Viva*, no. 27, Madrid, 1992.

[164.1]. Schachter, A. "Caving Out. Juan Navarro Baldeweg's Intellectual Poetry." *a+u,* no. 367, Tokyo, 2001.

[164.2]. — "One Exit in the Air and the Other in the Water: an Interview with Juan Navarro Baldeweg." *a+u,* no. 367, Tokyo, 2001.

[165]. Schulz-Dornburg, J. *Arte y arquitectura: nuevas afinidades. Juan Navarro Baldeweg, Casa de la Lluvia.* Barcelona: Gili, 2000.

[166]. Scortecci, V. "Altamira & Altamira." Juan Navarro Baldeweg, Altamira Musuem. *Lotus,* no. 103, Milan, 1999.

[167]. — "Il contrasto della luce e dell'ombra." Juan Navarro Baldeweg, Mahón Courthouse. *Lotus,* no. 102, Milan, 1999.

[168]. — "Sede della pretura, Mahón." *Domus*, no. 793, Milan, 1997.

[169]. — "Sede della Giunta dell'Estremadura a Merida." *Casabella*, no. 626, Milan, 1995.

[170]. Silveti, J. "Architecture's Outside. Juan Navarro Baldeweg." *Assemblage*, no. 34, MIT, Cambridge, MA, 1998.

[171]. Solà-Morales, I de. *Diferencias – Topografía de la arquitectura contemporánea.* Barcelona: Gili, 1995.

[172]. — "Light stone." *Images in Stone. Architecture in Stone International Award* . Milan: Electa, 1993.

[173]. — "La casa della pioggia (un proietto di Juan Navarro Baldeweg)." *Lotus International*, no. 44, Milan, 1984.

[174]. — See Rispa...

[175]. Solà-Morales, M. de. "Un'altra tradizione moderna. Dalla rottura dell'anno trenta al prog-etto urbano moderno." *Lotus International*, no. 64, Milan, 1990.

[176]. — "La segunda historia del proyecto urbano." *UR Urbanismo Revista*, no. 5, Barcelona, 1987.

[177]. Sustersic, P. "Juan Navarro Baldeweg. Centro Cultural en Villanueva de la Cañada." *Area*, no. 33, Milan, 1997.

[178]. Teyssot, G. "Interior Landscapes." *Quaderni di Lotus*, no. 8, Milan, 1986.

[179]. Thorne, M. "Juan Navarro Baldeweg." Interview. *Quaderns d'Arquitectura i Urbanisme*, no. 163, Barcelona, 1984.

[180]. Torrente Larrosa, A. "Juan Navarro Baldeweg." *Revista Cyan*, Madrid, 1988.

[181]. Torres i Estrade, J. "Navarro Baldeweg, el arte dentro del arte." *El Punto*, Barcelona, 1984.

[182]. Toto Shuppan. *581 Arquitectos en el mundo,* Gallery-ma, Tokyo, December 1995.

[183]. Trillo de Leyva, J. L. "La luz confinada: Letanía proyectada por Juan Navarro Baldeweg." *Periferia*, no. 7, Seville, 1987.

[184]. "Urbanización de la Rivera del Estadio, Balcón del Guadalquivir", "Rehabilitación del Molino de Martos." Córdoba between plans (1986–1999). *Geometría*, no. 25–26, Málaga, 1999.

[185]. Van Dijk, H: "Een monument uit een historiische leegte", *Archis*, no. 6, Rotterdam, 1993.

[186]. VV.AA: *Arquitectura española contemporánea. 1975–1990.* Madrid: El Croquis Ed., 1989.

[187]. Widder, L. "Princeton Music-. Die Erweiterung des Woolworth–Zentrums für Musik in Princeton." *Bauwelt*, no. 40–41, Berlin, 1999.

[188]. Woodward, C. "Wall, ceiling, enclousure and light: Soane's Designs for Domes." *John Soane Architect: Master of Space and Light.* London: Royal Academy of Arts, 1999.

[189]. Zabalbeascoa, A. "Entrevista a Juan Navarro." *Diseño Interior,* no. 85, Madrid, 1999.

[190]. — "Las grietas del tiempo. Concurso de la Ciudad de la Cultura de Galicia." *Arquitectura Viva*, no. 67, Madrid, 1999.

[191]. Zardini, M. "Destabilizzazioni e cataclismi." *Lotus*, no. 98, Electa, Milan, 1998.

[192]. — "Pochi lavori si sono presentati. Gli edifici di Juan Navarro Baldeweg a Madrid." *Lotus International*, no. 58, Milan, 1988.

Credits

Drawings
Juan Navarro Baldeweg

Plans
Juan Navarro Baldeweg and Juan Navarro Baldeweg Studio

Photographs
Photographic material provided by Juan Navarro Baldeweg Studio, sources and/or authors:
Aurofoto 155.3, 160.1
J. Azurmendi 45.3, 50.1, 54.1, 56.1, 56.2, 79.3, 81.5, 82-83, 84.1, 86.2, 87.5, 180.4
J. Bretón 150.1
F. Bucher 18.3, 106.2, 109.4, 111.4, 131.3, 132.2, 135.3, 181.1, 182.1, 182.2, 183.1a,
L. Casals 30-31, 33.2, 33.3, , 35.3, 35.4, 36.1, 178.2
N. Casla 137.3, 139.3, 141.1, 184.3
J.M. Churtichaga 25.3, 28.2, 177.1
Estudio Juan Navarro Baldeweg 13.1º, 13.4, 14.2, 119.2, 177.5, 178.3, 179.3, 179.4, 181.4
P. Fernández Lorenzo 189
A. Galmés / F. Bucher 99.2, 101.3, 103.4, 183.3a
J. García Rosell 10, 14.1, 16.3
R. González 47.3
R. Halbe 151.3, 153.4
A. Hernández 52-53
A. Jaque 15, 143.2, 145.4, 185.2
Jaque + Bernardini 159.3, 185.1
A. Levi 8, 17.1, 20.1, 20.2, 22, 113.2, 114.1, 117.3, 185.4186.1, 186.3
S. Lombardi Vallauri 136.1,
D. Malagamba 18.2, 19, 39.2, 40-41, 43.2, 49.3, 51.4, 59.3, 61.2, 63.5, 64.2, 67.3, 69.2, 71.3, 72-73, 77.2, 89.3, 90.3, 91.4, 93.4, 94-95, 97.2, 146-147, 163.2, 164.1, 166.2, 167.3, 169.4, 171.3, 172.1, 173.2, 173.4, 180.1, 182.3
I. Moreno 148.1, 153.5
J. Navarro Baldeweg 11, 12, 14.3, 16.1, 16.2, 176.1, 176.2, 176.3, 176.4, 176.5, 178.4, 178.5
J. Pando 120-121.1, 122.4, 123.5, 179.2, 183.2
E. Pujana 65.4
P. Roselli 178.1
C. San Millán / a+t 149.3
H. Suzuki 18.1, 55.4, 126.2